the Neuro-Psychology of Winning

© Copyright 2025– Denis Waitley and Deborah Waitley, PhD

All rights reserved. This book is protected by the copyright laws of the United States of America. No part of this publication may be reproduced, stored in or introduced into a retrieval system, or transmitted, in any form or by any means (electronic, mechanical, photocopying, recording or otherwise), without the prior written permission of the publisher. For permissions requests, contact the publisher, addressed "Attention: Permissions Coordinator," at the address below.

Published and distributed by:
SOUND WISDOM
P.O. Box 310
Shippensburg, PA 17257-0310
717-530-2122

info@soundwisdom.com

www.soundwisdom.com

While efforts have been made to verify information contained in this publication, neither the author nor the publisher assumes any responsibility for errors, inaccuracies, or omissions. While this publication is chock-full of useful, practical information; it is not intended to be legal or accounting advice. All readers are advised to seek competent lawyers and accountants to follow laws and regulations that may apply to specific situations. The reader of this publication assumes responsibility for the use of the information. The author and publisher assume no responsibility or liability whatsoever on the behalf of the reader of this publication.

The scanning, uploading and distribution of this publication via the Internet or via any other means without the permission of the publisher is illegal and punishable by law. Please purchase only authorized editions and do not participate in or encourage piracy of copyrightable materials.

ISBN 13 TP: 978-1-64095-571-4

ISBN 13 eBook: 978-1-64095-572-1

For Worldwide Distribution, Printed in the U.S.A.

1 2 3 4 5 6 7 8 / 29 28 27 26 25

Unlocking the Science of Peak Performance

the Neuro-Psychology of Winning

DENIS WAITLEY & DEBORAH WAITLEY, PHD

Dedication

To all who believe that each of us has the power to change our thoughts, our actions, our habits and the outcomes in our lives.

Acknowledgments

Our special thanks to Nathan Martin and John Martin, and the entire team at Sound Wisdom for their masterful, personal touch in every aspect of this book. They have transformed our research into a powerful life guide.

Contents

Chapter 1	Why The NeuroPsychology of Winning?	11
Chapter 2	Winning: The New Definition	33
Chapter 3	Living by Choice, Not Chance	51
Chapter 4	The Brain Train Revolution	65
Chapter 5	Reimagining Your Life	79
Chapter 6	Reprogramming Your Software	107
Chapter 7	Your Internal GPS: Goal Positioning System	121
Chapter 8	Habits: Our Invisible Robots	135
Chapter 9	Optimism: The Biology of Hope	151
Chapter 10	Resiliency: The Key to Success	171
Chapter 11	Empowerment and Relationships	187
Chapter 12	A Glimpse Into the Future	201
About the Authors		219

Chapter 1

Why The Neuro-Psychology of Winning?

In a fast-forward society, where change seems to be the only constant, it is increasingly important to pause and reflect on how we connect with each other on a personal level. Too often we rely on electronic impressions for feedback—the number of Facebook friends and followers, the size of our social media database, tweets, text messages, Instagrams, blogs, and virtual interactions. Our daily activities in "cyberspace" do create a permanent, indelible diary about ourselves that can be readily accessed by others now and in the future. To many individuals, their material rewards and status are their primary gauges of how successful they consider themselves to be. Others have immersed themselves into a world of avatars, in which they can enjoy the utopia of virtual friends, virtual pets, virtual possessions, virtual vacations, virtual lovers, and even virtual wealth.

We think this book—an updated print version of our audio program—can be a wake-up call. As the speed and ease of communications have increased exponentially, the "feelings of warmth," "intimacy," and "empathy" get lost in transmission. Traditions and values that once were universal guideposts for decency, civility, and being considerate of others are considered too old-fashioned and time consuming in an era where "urgency" rules. Our emotional impact on others is the key to developing a long-term, trusting relationship. We need to internalize the often repeated cliché, "No one cares how much you know, until they know how much you care." Emotions are the primary reasons behind almost every human transaction.

Our goal is to examine the melding of psychology and neuroscience and their impact on our daily lives and to share timely technological advancements with timeless wisdom gained from a lifetime of studying the whole person: brain, mind, body, and spirit.

What can't be transmitted electronically is how others feel and continue to feel about our interaction with them. There is no app for being "culture smart" or "mindful" as we navigate a world of human diversity—where diversity is more about what people believe than what you can see with your eyes. There are standards of decency, civility, and courtesy that should never change. Many of those standards are centuries' old in their origins and apply everywhere in the world. They relate more to how you present your best self to others, every day, wherever you are. This is why "emotional intelligence" is so important in building lasting relationships based on mutual respect and trust.

Several chapters in this book deal with specific actions you can take to rewire your brain to help make winning a habit, just like Olympians, astronauts, and gifted performers excel as a result of knowledge, skills, and practice. However, the underlying theme is to enhance your self-awareness in your interactions with others, both personal and professionals. We want you to be able to distinguish the difference between *"Artificial* Intelligence" and *"Authentic* Intelligence." We want you to give you the mental edge.

Back to Basics: Human Brain Function

During just the past decade, neuroscientists have learned more about human brain function than research had provided during the previous 50 years. As neuroscience researchers work to unravel the inner workings of the brain, we know more than ever about the mysteries of where emotions originate in the brain and the connections between instinct, intelligence, and emotion.

> # Train your brain to make winning a habit.

This work is yielding fascinating insights that we can use to understand how we react to situations and people. The brain, which is a much more flexible organ than previously thought, can be consciously rewired to be more emotional, trainable, understanding, and sensitive. At our Waitley Institute, my daughter, Deborah Waitley, who earned her PhD in transpersonal psychology, and I conducted research in the neuromarketing field several years ago to identify and measure brain activity related to consumer buying decisions and how to persuade others to buy into concepts and ideas.

We already know what behavior patterns influence people to say yes to what someone is trying to sell them, whether a product, service, or lifestyle. For example:

- People want a good deal, which equates to the most value for the lowest investment.

- However, people think high price means more value, which of course isn't necessarily true, but people pay more because they think they're getting more.

- People buy into celebrity endorsements somehow equating star status to expertise.

- People also respond favorably to common peer group endorsements, believing that if he or she can do it, so can I.

Getting Others to say "Yes" to You

One of the keys to getting others to trust you is to understand that most people say yes to people they know and like, especially if they deem them to be authority figures. And of course, there are many more obvious fixed-action behaviors including scarcity and time deadlines that drive decisions. Reciprocity means that people feel obligated to repay a favor. People bargain for needs and then splurge on wants, which is why reward motivation and inspiration are much more effective than fear motivation and intimidation.

> Reward motivation and inspiration are much more effective than fear motivation and intimidation.

People don't respond favorably, especially today, to coercion and hard-sell closing techniques. They want to feel that they're making their choices without outside pressure. With so much competition today, with so many distractions and so many options, the idea of closing a sale is obsolete—and the concept of *nurturing a long-term relationship is the secret to a winning team, customer retention, and innovation.*

And finally, we know that when it comes to sales, quotas, and goal setting, incremental steps work best because a minimum purchase leads to escalating commitments, just as small successes lead to increased confidence and risk-taking.

Recently, the melding of fixed-action behavioral psychology and neuroscience has become highly sophisticated with major corporations hiring neural research companies to understand buying behavior from a new perspective. Just as yesterday's world records are today's entry-level requirements, so too has a new tipping point been reached in understanding the secrets to motivating the emerging champions in our professional and personal lives.

There are many false assumptions concerning how our brains and minds function. We now have a truth for nearly every myth that has been passed on to us. And the following are just a few:

Myth: People make buy-in decisions in a rational, linear manner.

Truth: People's decisions are first influenced by emotional triggers and then by logic; emotions dominate the decision-making process.

Myth: People can readily explain their thinking and behavior.

Truth: People have far less access to their own mental activities than perceived. About 95 percent of thinking is an unconscious habitual process. Surveys and focus groups are often misused.

Myth: People's memories accurately represent their experiences.

Truth: People's memories are constantly changing without their awareness. Instead of a Facebook photo album, memory is more like a constantly edited music video full of fragments, real and imagined. As you are remembering something, your brain is in the process of rewiring the connections between neurons, which is actually changing the structure of your brain. Rather than video playback, your memory is more like video editing. Every time you remember something, you are changing, recreating, or rememorizing. A memory is subject to change every time you remember it. Hence, the term used by an aging athlete, "The older I get, the better I was." And the fisherman who remembers that the fish was as big as the boat.

Myth: People's talents are received at conception as natural gifts.

Truth: Although talents are inherited, new talents and abilities can be learned by retraining the brain.

Myth: We're born with a finite number of about 100 billion brain cells, and when one dies, a new one cannot grow. The ability to generate new neural pathways begins to decrease sharply around age 20.

Truth: Neuroscientists are learning more about neuro-plasticity, which is the ability of the brain to generate new neural cells and reorganize to form new neural pathways to adapt as needed. Neurogenesis, or the generation of new neurons, can continue throughout our lifespan even into old age, which is great news for me since I found my car keys in the refrigerator the other day. Surprisingly, millennials age 18 to 34 are more forgetful than baby boomers. They're more likely to forget what day it is or where they put their keys than their parents. I had to get that zinger in for my grandchildren. The creation of new neural pathways does take focused effort over time. However, the ability to rewire your brain to generate success and health-related pathways is at the forefront of individual and team peak performance.

Myth: People think in words.

Truth: Two-thirds of all brain stimuli are visual. Neural activities, thoughts precede their expression as words or language. Words and other senses can trigger thoughts, but thoughts are not words.

The following are the takeaway concepts from this previous discussion:

Why The NeuroPsychology of Winning?

- The decision to believe, agree, or buy-in is based upon a few basic pieces or even a single piece of reliable information that triggers a positive action.

- We should base coaching and training on current brain-mind science.

- We must consider the emotional triggers that motivate immediate positive responses to communications.

- We must motivate without perceived coercion. Instead of mass marketing to a general audience, we should embrace the concept of *me-marketing* to individuals because personalization will dominate all future transactions.

- Our communications and training should be interactive to personalize the relationship and lead to loyalty and retention.

- Our messages should be clear, brief, and to the point with immediate response options.

- We should focus on desired outcomes, not penalties of failure. We have the ability to edit and reprogram our bad memories so they don't hold us back. And we have the ability to edit and spruce up our good memories so they propel and launch us forward.

As you will discover while reading this book, you can engage in instant replay of positive memories with the ability to select and magnify your positive experiences to make yourself more resilient in trying times. You can also engage in instant *pre-play* of your goals and desires and create new neural pathways to channel your imaginations toward the winner's circle, realizing that your brain cannot distinguish between real experience and vividly imagined emotional passions internalized through constant practice.

We live in a fast-forward world with more changes in one of our days than in a decade of our grandparents' lives. Every five minutes, a new scientific research study is published involving some new technological or biotechnology discovery. Unfortunately, some of the most incredible technology wonders including television, the internet, amazing graphic motion pictures, and instant networking bombard our senses 24/7. The average brain has about 50,000 thoughts per day, and 70 percent of them are believed to be negative.

Media producers are paid well to know what sells. They know that the need to be shocked or viscerally stimulated is greater than the need to be informed or inspired. This same psychology is what makes a crowd gather at a fight or an accident. And neuroscience is in full swing on Madison Avenue. Slick emotional repetitions flow into our minds and the message is powerful. That message says that material goods and leisure activities are the only significant sources of happiness. We're led to believe that all of life's

Why The NeuroPsychology of Winning?

problems can be solved by products or services in about 60 seconds, which is why we become a skin-deep, immediate-gratification society. Fashion does not imitate real life. Life imitates fashion. The media shape our patterns of eating, sleeping, dressing, and recreation. They help form our values, morals, professional goals, social behavior, and perceptions of the real world.

> **Fashion does not imitate real life. Life imitates fashion.**

Unfortunately, too many of us exist on a mental diet of mental junk food. Not only is it addictive, but it also seems to produce an insatiable hunger for more, which leads to emotional malnutrition. The nutrition industry cautions us that we are what we eat, but we also become that to which we're most exposed, which means we are what we watch, listen to, and read. There are as many theories about the media blitz and learning as there are learners, but one thought is clear: we learn by observation, imitation, and repetition. We seize upon role models, observe their actions, imitate, and then become what we see, hear, read, feel, and touch, and no single realization is as important as this in understanding and dealing with your brain and mind.

Why Do We Do What We Do?

Later in the chapters that follow, we will discuss in more depth the constant bombardment of negative messages that foster pessimism, premonition and distress about the future. Catastrophes dominate all forms of media which pummel our senses in video streaming almost in real time. We are polarized politically, culturally and regionally.

There are several driving forces that dominate our lives:

- Bad news sells—viewership and ratings are driven by the shock effect.

- Fear is a powerful motivating force creating compulsion and inhibition.

- We act upon our current dominant thoughts, which through repetition become internalized in our brains as our reality.

- Fear can unwittingly become a goal when dwelled upon.

You can't concentrate on the reverse of an idea, which is like telling yourself what you don't want to happen. Imagine telling a child not to talk so much, not to be late or else, and not to believe in their own potential! As already mentioned, your brain can't distinguish real experience from vivid, repeated, emotion-laced images. The good news is that we have the answer to many of these roadblocks as we analyze the following riddle: *Why do we do what we do when we know what we know?* We know better than to fall into the trap of substance abuse, internalize unhealthy habits, procrastinate, alienate, prevaricate, yell, and lose composure over trifles, and on occasion engage in road rage.

So why do we do what we do when we know what we know? Because we don't always do what we know. We do what we've learned. And much of our learning takes place by unconscious modeling, observation, imitation, and repetition equals internalization. To whom have you given authority to train your brain in your current environment— the news or entertainment media, celebrities, friends and peers, tweets, and texts? Isn't it time to take control of your own future and train your brain to make winning your new habit? The answer is a resounding *yes*.

We at the Waitley Global Organization have never been as excited as we are with the launching of this book, *The NeuroPsychology of Winning*, and it's follow-on training and coaching programs. After years of experience in studying and working with astronauts, returning POWs, Olympians, Super Bowl and professional athletes, and peak performers in every field, we believe that the NeuroPsychology of

Winning can be a catalyst and launching pad for you, your team members, and inner circle.

Core Message

Our core message is this: *If no train, no gain—and if no brain train, your habits and performance will remain the same.* This NeuroPsychology of Winning program combines current breakthrough research in neuroscience and biotechnology with time-tested wisdom concerning peak performance and high achievement attitudes, behavior patterns, and actions. The result is a revolutionary brain-train program delivered in an easy-to-understand, easy-to-internalize format designed to increase motivation of individuals and team members to high-performance achievement in their business and personal lives.

This program will help you attract and retain customers and innovative professional team members by giving you the means to understanding emotional behavior triggers, subconscious responses to messaging, and how the brain and central nervous system operate synergistically.

You will also learn how to:

- View your mind as your internal software program containing attitudes, beliefs, and habits that can be overwritten to produce desired results.

Why The NeuroPsychology of Winning?

- Treat your brain and central nervous system as your physiological mission control center consisting of pre-programmed genetic data as well as data based on past and present life experiences that prevent you from or propel you toward completing your aspirations.

- Provide concise, useful, daily examples and action steps on how to lead yourself and others to more effective interpersonal and intrapersonal communications.

- Increase focus on primary priorities, a healthier, more optimistic view of the future, and how to handle setbacks, challenges, and difficult situations with resiliency and emotional intelligence.

Our mantras for the Psychology of Winning:

- There never was a winner who wasn't first a beginner.

- Winners believe in their dreams when that's all they have to hang on to.

- Winners deserve to win in advance.

- Winning is the feeling that you have no ceiling.

- Happiness cannot be traveled to owned, earned, worn, or consumed. Happiness is the spiritual experience of living every minute with love, grace, and gratitude.

We still believe and honor those statements as timeless wisdom. We know you're going to relish and benefit from what you're about to read. Timeless wisdom and timely neuroscience.

The Challenge

Our brains are flooded predominantly by external, negative inputs and stimuli, which is why our overreactions tend to be automatic fight or flight responses.

The good news is that our brains can be rewired to focus on positive outcomes, solutions, innovation and optimism. That is what excites us about breakthroughs in psychology and neuroscience.

Our brain cells are constantly talking to each other through chemical messaging. More than 100,000 chemical reactions take place in your brain every second. As we learn something new, our cells become more and more efficient about sending and receiving information about the task. The more we focus and practice, new neural connections are formed in the brain that help us sharpen our new skill. And once this new neural pathway is firmly established and strong, we don't need to focus our attention as much. New learning has become an automatic part of us, the same muscle memory reflex as with world-class athletes who perform effortlessly in the zone. Or when we view a masterful musical or dance performance that seems so spontaneous. Winning can become as natural as riding a bike or driving a car. *Practice makes permanent.*

It is a pleasure to add my voice and insights here and throughout this exciting new book of ours, *The NeuroPsychology of Winning,* as it is an updated print version of our audio program.

—**Deborah Waitley**

THE JOURNEY AHEAD

We've given you an introduction into why it's important to understand how the brain and our mind—this magnificent bio-network within—can work either for us, or against us. It comes down to the matter of how we choose to think, and therefore live. We are only given 24 golden hours in each precious day, and none of us know how many days we have ahead of us.

We do know we have today, and we are alive right now. How can we use what we currently have within us to make the most of *our* time?

ANOTHER MYTH TO CONSIDER

Here are some additional thoughts and another *myth* to consider: *We only use 10 percent of our brains.*

I was one of the millions who bought into this assumption years ago, possibly propagated by motivational speakers and trainers wanting to convince us to buy the quick-fix solutions they were selling. I even heard mention at one time that we only use 0.00001 percent of our brain.

The *reality* is that we use all parts—100 percent—of our brains, just not all at the same time, and definitely not as efficiently or effectively as we could. It is such a vast and complex system of different regions, functions, and pathways, that work together for our thinking, learning, creativity, problem-solving, and intelligence (cognitive and emotional).

For this body of work, we are taking a holistic approach to our merging of psychology with neuroscience, yet also generalizing and simplifying it this way:

Brain, *Our Hardware* – the structure that operates through electrical and chemical signals.

Mind, *Our Software* – our thoughts, consciousness and perceptions, which includes our reasoning, memory, imagination and emotions.

We know that the brain and mind are both interconnected and dependent on each other. The mind needs the brain to function, because as we know, any damage to the brain alters thoughts, personality, and emotions. Yet also, mental states (our thoughts and emotions) influence the brain's structure, neural network and chemistry throughout the body over time, as we know through research on plasticity and rewiring).

It is important to consider the ongoing relationship between the conscious and sub-conscious mind, as well as how the interplay between our "higher mind" and "lower mind" factors into our ability to respond and adapt to the world around us. We will be providing you with these foundational concepts, (specifically in Chapter 4), to help further your understanding of the brain/mind dynamics involved in how we navigate life's challenges.

WHAT DOES THIS MEAN FOR YOU?

We want to bring you the very best of what we know through our lifetime of work and research, so you can live your very best life. And this life is not one that imitates "fashion," but fashions itself out of your own unique qualities and characteristics, and allows you to live according to your greatest potential.

In the next chapter, we explore what it means to "win" in life, authentically. And in subsequent chapters, we will take you on a journey for ways to make this possible...through commitment, motivation, discipline, habit change, belief in yourself, effective goal-setting, visualization, positive self-talk, resiliency, empowerment, and optimism

Your flight path is set.

Now it's time for liftoff.

It's *your* time to *win!*

Reflect and Connect

At the end of each chapter, you will have the opportunity to "Reflect and Connect" with questions designed to stimulate further exploration.

Through the process of *reflecting* on new information, especially as it applies to your own life experiences—past and present—our capacity for deeper understanding and long-term retention is enhanced. Knowledge can become more meaningful as we begin *connecting* and assimilating new insights with tangible action, bringing about undreamed-of possibilities and lasting change.

1. Do you believe you *can* change your current trajectory to live your very best life?

2. How strong is your *desire* to change?

3. What has held you back in the past?

Chapter 2

Winning: The New Definition

Winning used to mean beating the others and being number one at any cost. Winning signified standing victoriously over a fallen adversary, the survival of the fittest. While it is true that there is only one Superbowl, World Cup, World Series champion crowned after each season, that doesn't mean that to come in second or third signifies a losing season.

Remember the slick TV commercial that tried to convince us that you don't win silver, you lose gold? The win-lose philosophy that suggests that there must be a loser for every winner, that winning by intimidation is fashionable, is obsolete. Instead of I win, you lose, the new definition must be *let's win together*. The real winners in the present and future world arena will be more often the champions of cooperation rather than merely competition. The win-win philosophy is the only one that can endure.

Win-win means if I help you win, then I win too. We're not suggesting that competition is bad—just the opposite. Competition keeps the quality standards high at a fair market price. Olympians compete against world class standards and the team events mean just as much to the participants as the individual events.

True winners get what they want by helping others get what they want. Independence has been replaced by inter-dependence. There are too many people, too few resources, and too delicate a balance between nature and technology to produce winners in isolation today. We are interdependent in terms of security and survival. We have the capacity to thrive together or perish together.

We must face the inescapable fact that we as individuals are a vital but single organ of a larger body of human beings in the world. The one cannot succeed or even survive for long anymore without the others. Instant access to information erases all boundaries except those that are cemented in our brains.

Three Major Hurdles

After all, what's so hard about applying if I help the other person win, I win too? Actually quite a bit. Before we can successfully practice win-win precepts, we have to recognize three major hurdles that stand in our way.

- One, the win-lose philosophy is natural.

- Two, the win-lose philosophy is dominant in our society.

- And three, the win-lose philosophy is habit-forming and addicting.

We live in a culture that is basically dedicated to the win-lose philosophy. It's a point of view that has become natural for us, and no one blames you for looking out for number one, as long as you're discreet and law-abiding about it.

Some adults live their entire lives at the emotional level that ranges from childlike to adolescent. The chief symptom? Preoccupation with the immediate gratification of self and its senses. The child's rationale is an uninhibited, if it feels good, do it. And the adolescent approach climbs a bit higher on the ladder to say, if it feels good, do it as long as you don't hurt anybody else.

The adolescent rationale is held by many adults who go their win-lose way doing what comes naturally. The admission that win-lose living is natural doesn't mean that it's healthy or that it will help society thrive and endure in the long run. Earthquakes, floods, anger, violence, and the fight or flight response are also natural, though not necessarily healthy phenomenon.

Win-Lose Versus Win-Win

Some tip-offs that reveal the win-lose approach include caring for others only to the extent that those others provide you with self-gratification. *What can she do for me?* Enjoying relationships only as long as they do not compromise selfish needs. *I'll love you if or when.* And withdrawing into materialism, the possession of things, which creates the fantasy of success in a vain hope to banish frustration and emptiness. *Yes, I paid a bundle for it, but it's only money.* Wanting to pay as little as possible for pleasure and fulfillment. *There must be a free ride in this somewhere.*

The win-win lifestyle is the antithesis of these attitudes. In fact, more than two decades ago, evolutionary biologists and psychologists began finding neural and possible genetic predispositions to cooperation rather than selfishness. The win-win person is prepared to pay the price of some self-deprivation in the cause of caring for others. Yet, no one is capable of giving love unconditionally all the time because the natural win-lose, look-out-for-number-one attitude is always in the way.

But an encouraging sign of true maturity and love is that you're increasingly willing to devote more time and effort to caring for others than trying to satisfy your own real or imagined needs. This is the win-win philosophy, and it doesn't come naturally. Authentic winners are those individuals who in a very natural, free-flowing way, seem to consistently get what they want from life by providing valuable service to others.

> # Authentic winners consistently get what they want from life by providing valuable service to others.

Authentic winners put themselves together across the board in their personal, professional, and community lives. They set and achieve goals that benefit others as well as themselves. You don't have to get lucky to win at life, nor do you have to knock other people down or gain at the expense of others.

Winning is taking the talent or potential you were born with and it was since developed, and using it fully toward a purpose that makes you feel worthwhile according to your own internal standards. Happiness then is the natural by-product of living a worthwhile life. Happiness is the natural experience of winning your own self-respect as well as the respect of others.

Even in this fast-forward world, some things never change. The old saying: "You never get a second chance to make a first impression," is more relevant today than it was during the early years of my career. In the 1980s, I remember reading a popular book titled, *Contact: The First Four Minutes,* by Leonard Zunin, MD. It was considered a must-read for everyone engaged in customer service and also advised that—in our interaction with those close to us and potential life partners—the first few minutes spent with them on a daily basis were critical to promoting mutual understanding. It is in this brief period that the decision is made to part or continue the encounter.

As computing and communication speeds have increased dramatically, so too have our brain's abilities to process incoming stimuli from the environment, including interpreting non-verbal and verbal signals from others. Today, instead of the first few minutes creating a lasting impression, it seems that the first few seconds of initial contact produce the same results.

Emotional Intelligence: The Winning Edge

The common thread throughout this book is all about enhancing our Emotional Intelligence (EQ)—our ability to manage and control our emotions, as well as influence the emotions of others. It requires honest self-awareness about our own beliefs and values, as well as our talents, personalities, and empathy in dealing with others.

As we have discovered, emotional intelligence is not normally a skill that we are taught. It is more often "caught" by trial and error on our life journeys. From our first encounter with others it was more about pushing the right hot buttons of their desires, while not pushing their built-in, defensive hot buttons. Establishing rapport, asking questions more than presenting, gaining trust and expressing genuine interest in creating an ongoing relationship—rather than pursuing our own selfish desires—resulted in more success and repeat business than any scripted techniques.

Likeability, encompasses those essential values of openness, transparency, trustworthiness, and reliability, along with a certain magnetism and an interest in others. It drives the ability to form and build on networks and alliances, exercise persuasiveness, gain credibility, and attract and retain talented team members.

Academic research suggests that an individual's emotional intelligence (EQ) is at least as important as his or her general intelligence and technical skills when it comes to being equipped for business and personal success—with some suggesting it's actually much more important. The good news is that, contrary to popular belief, likeability can be learned. Whether you are an introvert or extrovert, shy or gregarious, it's based entirely on your ability to recognize and control your emotions, and to understand and influence the emotions of others. It's easy to see how that could give you an edge in business.

Forbes has cited Emotional Intelligence as the #1 leadership skill for 2024 and beyond, according to the World Economic Forum's Future of Jobs 2023 report.[1] Qualities associated with emotional intelligence such as self-awareness, adaptability, continuous learning, motivation, and empathy are highly valued by businesses and will continue to be so for the foreseeable future.

Many of the top companies in the world, including Google, Amazon, Microsoft, Visa, Samsung, Nike, Netflix and Disney, are prioritizing Emotional Intelligence, a person's EQ, in their recruitment process. Using assessments that measure a potential employee's relationship management skills, their ability to perceive, understand, and manage emotions, as well as manage stress are just some of the determinants of success on the job.

The following are a few statistics that make for a compelling case for the value of having and developing a high EQ:

- Emotional intelligence is a better predictor of career success than IQ.

- Can predict more than 75% of job success.

---

1. Rachel Wells, "Emotional Intelligence No.1 Leadership Skill For 2024, Says Research," *Forbes,* January 5, 2024; https://www.forbes.com/sites/rachelwells/2024/01/05/emotional-intelligence-no1-leadership-skill-for-2024-says-research/; accessed February 28, 2025.

- Predicts 67% of a leader's effectiveness.

- 90% of the best performers have high emotional intelligence.

- Employees with high emotional intelligence perform 127% better than those with low emotional intelligence.

- Emotional intelligence explains 90% of what sets top performers apart from their peers.

- Companies that focus on hiring and training emotionally intelligent employees experience 22% more revenue growth.

- Emotional intelligence accounts for up to 70% of a person's overall success in life.

For these reasons, many top universities are now building Emotional Intelligence courses into their degree curriculums, which include Yale, Harvard, Cornell, and the University of Southern California.

Not only are companies hiring and training on Emotional Intelligence competencies, they are also measuring employee performance based on customer service feedback ratings. It is proven that customer behavior is driven by his or her perception of something that makes them emotional in a positive or negative way.

Empathy: An Emotional Intelligence Centerpiece

Understanding the difference between sympathy and empathy is a centerpiece for this entire book, which is why most of the chapters that follow are centered on the emotional intelligence we need to become successful in dealing with everyone we encounter every day.

Both *sympathy* and *empathy* have roots in the Greek term *pathos,* meaning, "suffering" or "feeling." Sympathy is mainly used today to convey commiseration, pity, or feelings of sorrow for someone who's experiencing misfortune. Just look at greeting cards labeled "sympathy" to understand what it means. Those cards specialize in messages of support and sorrow for others in a time of need. You feel badly for them...but you don't really know what it's like to feel how they do in that moment of pain or grief. Sympathy also can mean that you invest in someone else's cause, or take another's cause as your own.

Empathy, on the other hand, is the ability to imagine yourself in the situation of another, experiencing their emotions or concerns as if they were your own.

An example of learned empathy is a true story about a mother who had taken her four-year-old son to a large department store during the holiday season. She knew it would be fun for him to see all the decorations and interactive toys. As she dragged him by the hand, twice as fast as his little legs could move, he began to fuss and cry. She admonished him, saying, "We won't go shopping together if you keep this up." Then she noticed that his shoes were untied. "Oh, maybe it's because you're tripping over your own laces," she said, kneeling down in the aisle to tie his shoes.

As she knelt down beside him, she happened to look up. For the first time, she saw a large department store through the eyes of a four-year-old. From that position, there were no decorations, animated displays or toys, or piles of goodies. All she could see was a maze of corridors too high to see above, full of giant shopping carts! Mountainous strangers, with feet as big as skateboards, were pushing and shoving, bumping and thumping, rushing and crushing on their way to the checkout counter.

Rather than fun, the scene looked terrifying. She took her child home, and vowed never to impose her version of a good time on him again.

Empathy means to walk in another's shoes before passing judgment.

Deborah ~

In the early days of my training and consulting career, Emotional Intelligence was frowned upon and not considered to be a viable factor in performance success. However, many years later, the bulk of my client engagements involved EQ coaching and development. It was previously thought that EQ traits such as empathy were primarily the result of innate genetic predispositions. We now know that with the right environmental and motivational factors, individuals can be trained to learn empathy and other interpersonal EQ skills, and over time, even develop them enough to become part of one's personality.

Much of my corporate work involved training and coaching leaders on how to boost customer service performance within their sales teams. We saw significant improvement in customer satisfaction scores, when we focused on developing empathy. This was particularly evident in call centers, where agents had to communicate empathy solely through their phone voice. So without the advantages of eye contact and in-person presence, sales agents learned to convey empathy through the tone of their voice, inflection and the use of specific "supportive" words, that made the customers feel validated and heard. Interestingly, the individuals who were most successful in developing greater empathy, demonstrated significant improvement in their own job satisfaction and engagement scores, as well as higher levels of motivation and productivity. Not surprisingly, they also self-reported that they experienced noticeable positive changes in their personal lives!

Happiness Is a Decision, Not a Result

As mentioned in Chapter 1, you can't buy happiness, wear it, drive it, swallow it, inject it, or travel to it. Happiness is the journey, not the destination. We're in a fast-forward world where there are no timeouts, no substitutions, and the clock is always running. The choices we make in response to our circumstances, the goals we set, and the actions we take on a daily basis determine to a large extent the outcomes in our lives. True enough, we don't control the cards we're dealt in terms of genetics, geography, upbringing, and natural disasters along with the unavoidable actions by others.

However, we alone play the hand that we've been dealt and we survive and thrive by the wisdom of our own decisions. It's not what happens to you in life that counts. It's how you take it and what you make of it. It's true. Things turn out best for the people who make the best of the way things turn out. Winning has a different meaning for every individual. You spend your life learning, exploring, growing, losing, winning, and if you're unselfish, trying to make a positive contribution. Your life is a collection of moments and memories.

> # You survive and thrive by the wisdom of your own decisions.

Your Legacy

Life also consists of the legacy that you pass on to family and future leaders. The lessons you leave in your own next generation as core values are far more priceless than the material valuables you'll leave them in your estate. Life is governed by universal laws that remain unchanged since the beginning of recorded time. Actions cause reactions, rights carry responsibilities, truth promotes trust, thoughts become things, love is to life as the sun is to planet Earth, and *every choice carries a reward or consequence.*

Winning: The New Definition

In the long run like rings within a tree, each of us becomes the sum total of our actions. There are pros and cons concerning our preoccupation with cyber life. To a certain extent, technology is the enemy of intimacy, in that a smiley-face text often replaces face-to-face interaction, and cell phone selfies, Facebook posts, Instagrams and X/Tweets can be self-centered methods of displaying self-importance rather than bringing out the best in others.

Critics are calling today's culture, "the age of human robots living in a virtual world." I prefer to see technology for its positive opportunities. Fortunately, social media and advanced technologies provide a real-time network that allows us to share opinions, celebrate diversity, and promote inclusion—especially of those from cultures with beliefs and worldviews different from our own.

It's possible that authentic cornerstones for living successfully that transcend all borders and prejudices can go viral and permeate the consciousness of succeeding generations. In our virtual work lives and geographically challenged personal relationships, technology helps us stay connected with loved ones and friends, work teams, peers, and colleagues whom we otherwise would not have an opportunity to see face to face. The key takeaway message here is that every electronic connection that we make via Facebook, YouTube, X/Twitter, Instagram, blog, and every email and text projects our beliefs and actions as well as the opinions of those we encounter.

47

These electronic impressions begin to reflect a perceived brand identity or persona about ourselves that could become reality—which are stored and cannot be erased. And just as the internet stores a permanent record of all your communications, negative and positive, so too does your brain store everything you've ever experienced, real or imagined. Emotional inputs are especially powerful and dominating.

Override, Rewrite, Rewire

However, they can never willfully be erased. The exciting news is that we can override, rewrite, and actually rewire our brains to turn losing habits into winning actions and high-performance achievements. In the next chapter, you will learn how this is possible. The greatest men and women in all walks of life achieve their greatness out of a desire to express something within themselves that had to be expressed.

Successful people, successful in the deepest sense of the word, don't look for achievements that will bring them the most for the least amount of effort. They look for the greatest challenges to test their potential.

In considering your own potential, realize that success and fulfillment choices in your life far exceed what you may currently think is possible. And our concept of possible is always expanding. Scientists at the Salk Institute for

Biological Studies in La Jolla, California, discovered that the memory storage capacity of our brains is 10 times more than what they had previously thought. The memory storage capacity is a "petabyte," which is the equivalent of 500 billion pages of text. This begs the question, "What are you storing in your mental library?"

Do not limit your thinking. Do not impose mental obstacles before you give yourself and your brain an opportunity to explore possibilities—and believe in the winner in you.

> **Successful people look for the greatest challenges to test their potential.**

Reflect and Connect

1. What does the concept of "Winning" mean to you? How would you define it, for yourself, in your own life?

2. How influenced are you by the ways in which "Winning" is defined in our current society, culture, and by others in your life?

3. How closely aligned are your personal values with those of your friends, work associates and organization, and the world at large?

4. Do you consider yourself to be an empathetic person? How could you improve?

Chapter 3

Living by Choice, Not Chance

Think of yourself as an astronaut on an amazing lifetime journey into the unknown. Your life so far has been a training experience preparing you for what lies ahead. You've had your share of mistakes and successes. Technological advances have created unimaginable opportunities for fulfillment and also have overwhelmed your senses with constant change and complexity. You are relying on your own personal perceptions and beliefs, some of which have become invisible barriers causing uncertainty.

Think of your brain as your mission control center. It makes decisions with or without your conscious awareness. More than you realize, you can rewire the communication network to set a new course of actions to turn dreams into reality.

Peak performers don't blame past conditioning or circumstances for their actions. Their decisions are results of their own choices based on core values and knowledge. Our actions cause consequences. "For every action," as Sir Isaac Newton observed, "there is an equal and opposite reaction." Good begets good and evil leads to more evil. This is one of the universe's eternal, fundamental truths: the law of cause and effect.

It means that every cause (action) will create an effect (reaction) approximately equal in intensity. Making good use of our minds, skills, and talents will bring positive rewards in our outer lives. Assuming the personal responsibility to make the best use of our talents and time will result in an enormous gain in happiness, success, and wealth. In a very real sense, we all become hostages of hundreds of restrictions of our own choosing or with the assistance of the entertainment media, peers, and our parents.

Self-determination is what separates the winners from the losers in business, sports, and life. Are you someone who perseveres no matter the challenges or setbacks? Or do you throw in the towel and quit when adversity strikes? By changing our attitude and behavior, we have the power to increase the production of our most valuable natural resource, dopamine—the fuel that keeps us motivated to persevere when the going gets tough.

Research has shown there are two fundamental belief systems or "mindsets" that determine how we respond to obstacles, setbacks, and failure in pursuit of our goals. With a "fixed mindset" you're likely to become easily discouraged and give up on a goal, as you believe there isn't much you can do to change the human qualities you were born with.

With a winning "growth mindset" you're more apt to embrace struggles and learn from adversity to fuel you forward. You see your human qualities and traits are abilities you can further develop through hard work, education, and practice. You choose to take responsibility for your success through positive self-determination and perseverance!

Coaches and mentors influence our success. However, we alone, as individuals, make the choice and take the responsibility for giving up bad habits and invalid assumptions.

The Price of Success

The price of success includes:

- Taking responsibility for giving up bad habits and invalid assumptions.

- Taking responsibility for setting an example in our own lives.

- Distancing ourselves from a peer group that isn't helping us succeed and therefore tends or wants to hold us back.

- Leading ourselves and others down a new and unfamiliar path.

- Working more to reach a goal and being willing to delay gratifications along the way.

- Being willing to face criticism and jealousy from people who would like to keep us stuck in place with them.

- Understanding that we can train our brains and rewire our neural pathways to develop new habits for peak performance.

These are among the perceived costs of success that prompt people to escape from the present by occupying their minds with past memories or future expectations. Leaders, by contrast, are not dismayed by the cost of success. They get started and build positive momentum. Top corporate leaders are recognizing the value of creating a culture of excellence by facilitating the "growth mind-set" throughout their workforce. Just as companies must dissolve their boundaries and erase their hierarchies, so must you, the individual, reinvent yourself to meet the knowledge era's changing demands.

What this means is that you're your own chief executive officer. Start thinking of yourself as a service company with a single employee. You're a small company—very small, but that doesn't matter—that puts your services to work for a larger company. Tomorrow you may sell those services to a different organization, but that doesn't mean you're any less loyal to your current employer. You're your own

CEO who must have the vision to set your own goals and allocate your resources in your business and personal life to become more productive. This mindset will help you take charge of your future, starting today.

It means that every cause (action) will create an effect (reaction) approximately equal in intensity. Making good use of our minds, skills, and talents will bring positive rewards in our outer lives. Assuming the personal responsibility to make the best use of our talents and time will result in an enormous gain in happiness, success, and wealth.

This is true of everyone. However, scarcely one person in a thousand puts his or her time to anywhere near its potential good use. Most of us fritter away much of our lives watching the game from the sidelines. Nor is there any ultimate advantage in taking praise or rewards away from others.

Every time we think we can cheat our boss, fellow workers, friends, and family members, or peers, we hurt ourselves most of all. Every less-than-properly-responsible act toward others slashes most deeply into our own opportunity to grow and prosper.

The truly successful leaders, those who have accomplished great deeds for society, are those who have been taking personal responsibility to heart and to soul. By being true to themselves and others, they achieve success, wealth, and inner happiness.

And in the end, we ourselves—far more than any outsider—are the people with the greatest ability to steal our own time, talents, and accomplishments. In a very real sense, we all become hostages of hundreds of restrictions of our own choosing. As children we either accepted or rejected teachings and lifestyles of the significant adults in our lives.

As the father of four children, seven grandchildren, and four great-grandchildren, I know from personal experience that the greatest gifts that parents can give their children (and that managers can give their employees) are roots and wings. Roots of responsibility and wings of independence. When those roots and wings are missing, the results are very disturbing—even tragic.

In our parenting and leadership seminars, I tell a true story about a young couple who invited me to their home for dinner some time ago after an all-day program at a university.

This man and woman were both highly intelligent, with advanced degrees, but they'd opted for a "child-centered" home so that their five-year-old son Bradford would have everything at his disposal to become a winner out there in the competitive world. When I arrived at their driveway in front of a fashionable two-story home, I should have known what was in store for me.

I stepped on one of Bradford's many scattered toys getting out the car and was greeted by, "Watch where you're walking, Mister, or you'll have to buy me new ones!"

Entering the front door, I instantly discovered that this was Bradford's place, not his parents' home. The furnishings, it appeared, were originally of fine quality before their son practiced his demolition skills on them.

We attempted to have a cup of tea in the family room, but Bradford was busy ruining his new video game controls. Trying to find a place to sit down was like hopping on one foot through a minefield, blindfolded. Bradford was the first to be served with food, in the living room, so that he wouldn't be lonely.

I nearly dropped my hot cup of tea in surprise when they brought out a highchair that was designed like an aircraft ejection seat with four legs and straps.

He was five years old and had to be strapped in a highchair to get through one meal! (Soon, I wished it had been a real aircraft ejection seat!) As we started eating our salads, young Bradford dumped his dinner on the carpet and proceeded to pour his milk on top of it to ensure that the peas and carrots would go deep into the shag fibers. His mother entreated, "Brad, honey, don't do that. Mommy wants you to grow up strong and healthy like Daddy. I'll get you some more dinner while Daddy cleans it up."

While they were occupied with their chores, Bradford had unfastened his seat belts, scrambled down from his perch, and joined me in the dining room, helping himself to my olives. "I think you should wait for your own dinner," I said politely, removing his hand from my salad bowl. He swung his leg up to kick me in the knee, but my old ex-pilot reflexes didn't fail me, and I crossed my legs so quickly that he missed, came off his feet and came down hard on the floor on the seat of his pants.

You'd have thought he was at the dentist's office. He screamed and ran to his mother, sobbing, "He hit me!" When his parents asked what happened, I calmly informed them that he had fallen accidentally and I muttered quietly under my own breath to myself (besides, "I'd never hit the head of a household!").

I knew it was time to be on my way when they put their little prince to bed, by placing granola cookies on the stairs as enticers. And he ate his way up to bed!

"How are you ever going to motivate him to go to school?" I asked quietly. "Oh, I'm sure we'll come up with something," they laughed. "Yes, but what if the neighborhood dogs eat what you put out? He'll lose his way just like Hansel and Gretel!" The couple didn't find that humorous and never invited me back.

As traveling lecturers, Deborah and I have seen many children worldwide who are in charge of their parents and we also have observed many teenagers and adults who, as a result of overly permissive or overly strict leadership at home, are out of control.

Life's greatest risk is being spoiled or pampered and then feeling entitled to depend on others for your security, which can really come only by planning, acting, and making choices that will make you independent. Leadership ideas that solve problems and create opportunity come from creative trial-and-error thinking.

Years of study and some painful personal experiences have convinced us that the fear of the costs of success are among the reasons that prejudiced people resist change.

What this means is that you're your own chief executive officer.

So, start thinking of yourself as a service company with a single employee. You're a small company—very small, but that doesn't matter—that puts your services to work for a larger company. Tomorrow you may sell those services to a different organization, but that doesn't mean you're any less loyal to your current employer.

The first step is resolving not to suffer the fate of those who lost their jobs and found their skills were obsolete and the second is to begin immediately the process of protecting yourself against that possibility—by becoming proactive instead of reactive.

So, ask yourself how vulnerable you are and what you can do about it.

"What trends must I watch? What information must I gain? What knowledge do I lack?" Again, think of yourself as a company—for this purpose a research and development company—and establish your own strategic planning department. Set up a training department and make sure your top employee is updating his or her skills. Start your own investment plan knowing that you are responsible for your own financial security.

You're your own CEO who must have the vision to set your goals and allocate your resources. Since your primary concern is ensuring your viability in the marketplace, you must think strategically in every decision.

This mindset of being responsible for your own future used to be crucial only for the self-employed, but it has become essential for us all. For today's typical workers are no longer one-career people. Most will have several separate careers in their lifetimes. But although you must become your own life's CEO and always act as if you were a company of one, being a team leader is equally important for your future. It's no longer possible to achieve alone in our world of accelerating change, where the new global village has become the local neighborhood.

Rather than become dependent on others, however, we should become interdependent, treating everyone we meet as a potential customer, someone with whom we may develop a strategic alliance in the future.

The Seven "Cs" of Control

Although many things in life are beyond anyone's control, you do have a great deal of control—more than most of us are willing to acknowledge—over many of the circumstances and conditions.

1. You can control the Clock, what you do with most of your free time during the day and the evening.

2. You can control your Concepts and imagination, channeling what you think about.

3. You can control your Contacts, who you spend your leisure time with—and, to a great degree, your colleagues.

4. You can control your Communications. You can choose to remain silent or choose to speak. If you choose to speak, you can choose your words and your tone of voice.

5. You can control the Causes to which you give your time and goals. And this is what we call the "purpose behind the purpose."

6. You can control your Concerns and worries and whether you will choose to take action about them, as well as your response to difficult times and people.

7. You can control your Commitments, the things you absolutely promise yourself and others that you will do.

Key Action Ideas

We encourage you to adopt the following actions into your daily walk:

- Carry this affirmative motto with you: My rewards in life will reflect my service and contributions.

- Set your own standards rather than comparing yourself to others. Successful people know they must compete with themselves, not with others. They run their own races.

- Use another motto for your self-analysis: Life is a do-it-yourself project. When your subordinates or teammates bring you a problem, first ask them what they think they should do and what should be done to resolve it. Be certain to assign responsibility for the solution and follow through to the subordinate or team member. Resist taking the easy way out by doing it for them.

- Let your teammates, subordinates, and your children make mistakes without fear of punishment or rejection. Show them that mistakes are learning devices that become steppingstones to success.

- Break your daily and weekly routine. Get out of your comfortable rut. Unplug the TV for a month. Take a different route or different mode of transportation to work. Have lunch with people in totally different industries and read publications in totally different fields from your current one.

Emotional Security

To achieve emotional security, each of us must develop two critical abilities:

1. The ability to live with change and uncertainty.

2. And the ability to delay immediate gratification for the sake of long-term goals.

Learn to take more personal responsibility for your choices in life by practicing the simple urgings in the "Serenity Prayer" by Reinhold Niebuhr: "God, grant me the serenity to accept the things I cannot change, the courage to change the things I can, and the wisdom to know the difference."

This means that I "accept the unchangeable!" which is everything that has already happened. That's history and cannot be changed. So, I harbor my pleasant memories and gain perspective from the problems in my past.

My only control is to "change the changeable!" which is my response to what has happened and my decisions in this present moment in time; to accept with serenity what has happened and courageously taking positive action in the here and now.

Reflect and Connect

Consider a challenging situation you are currently experiencing in your life, and answer the following questions:

1. Are you able to identify and accept which things are beyond your control? And then move on to what you *can* change?

2. What aspects are within your ability to change; specifically, your thoughts and feelings about the situation?

3. How willing and committed are you to make these changes?

Chapter 4

The Brain Train Revolution

The brain train *evolution* in just the past decade has become more of a *revolution,* than a slow evolution. It's one thing to know that you can program yourself for success and another almost impossible task to understand how and why. The brain is extremely complex. All human inventions including the computer, spacecraft, smartphones, and medical devices are toys in comparison. Nuclear physicist George Edgin Pugh wrote in his 1977 book, *The Biological Origin of Human Values,* a statement that pretty well sums it up, "If the brain were so simple that we could understand it, we would be so simple that we couldn't."

We're only just beginning to discover the virtually limitless capacities of the brain, and we've learned more about how the brain functions during the past decade than in much of the past century.

How Your Brain Functions

Without getting too technical, you should understand a few critical concepts of how your brain functions. In an oversimplification, your brain is divided into two major components, the cerebral cortex or upper part of the brain and the *sub cortex* or lower part. Every day scientists are discovering new capabilities of the brain that make previous theories outdated or obsolete.

The *subcortical* (sub cortex) areas of the brain house your feelings and emotions. They compose the basic control center for the autonomic body functions such as breathing, heart rate, blood vessel diameters, and body temperature, functions that for decades were considered involuntary. Today we know that we can exert a degree of conscious control over these functions through the use of neurofeedback, biofeedback, relaxation, and certain imagery techniques.

The *cerebral cortex* houses our higher-order thinking or intelligence functions such as language, memory, and judgment. This bulging mass of nervous tissue is what we generally see when the brain is pictured. It's divided into two hemispheres, the left and the right. Most researchers concur that the left hemisphere, which controls the right side of the body, contains many of the verbal, logical, and analytical functions. The right hemisphere, which controls the left side of the body, functions as the visual, intuitive, and holistic partner.

> **The brain's left hemisphere controls the body's right side and contains verbal, logical, and analytical functions. The right hemisphere controls the body's left side as the visual, intuitive, and holistic partner. We depend on the seamless cooperation and communication between both sides to function optimally.**

My personal experience as an eager student of the evolution of NeuroPsychology occurred in the late 1960s while I was working as a non-scientist at the Salk Institute for Biological Studies in my hometown of La Jolla, California. I recall learning that some of the exciting breakthroughs concerning the brain began in the 1960s when Dr. Roger Sperry and his students initiated their split-brain experiments.

In these studies, they were able to test separately the mental abilities of the two surgically separated hemispheres of the human brain, and they discovered that each half of the brain has its own separate train of conscious thought and its own memories. More importantly, they found that each side thinks in fundamentally different ways, the left brain thinking in words and the right brain thinking directly in pictures and feelings.

Most of our awake lives are under the conscious control of our left brain. When we are blessed with a great idea or a flash of insight, it seems to arrive suddenly and in a surprisingly complete form. Apparently it was incubating unconsciously in our right brain.

Musical geniuses Mozart and Beethoven said they heard symphonies in their heads and only had to write them down from memory. What has always amazed me is the research reported during brain surgery in which patients whose brain cells were stimulated with a thin electrode, described the sensation of reliving scenes from the past. Their recall was so strong and vivid that all details were there again—sounds, colors, people, shapes, places, and odors. *They were not just remembering but reliving the experiences.*

Just as our bodies react to our own memories as well as images from the external world, our bodies also react to our own *imagined* experiences or rehearsals. American physiologist Edmund Jacobson conducted studies showing that when a person imagines running, small but measurable amounts of contraction actually take place in the leg muscles. In the same way, when you create a vivid frightening image in your mind, your body responds with a quickened pulse, elevated blood pressure, sweating, goose bumps, and dryness of the mouth.

Conversely, when you hold a strong, positive, relaxing image in your mind, your body responds with a lowered heart rate and decreased blood pressure, and all your muscles tend to relax. These functions take place automatically, unconsciously, and you're seldom aware of their cause. You think they just happened.

Brain Resilience and Regenerative Capacity

Until recently, we've underestimated the resilience and regenerative capacity in the human brain. People recovering from strokes and other brain injuries have demonstrated the remarkable capacity of the brain to regenerate. When parts of the brain have been destroyed or damaged, remaining parts can come to the rescue and learn how to take over functions that were lost.

For example, when an injury occurs to the left hemisphere, which controls our language and speech, mirror neurons located in the right side of the brain can become involved in those functions. Recovering patients who can't speak but can still hum a song, can learn to associate words and phrases with melodies, helping them with communications. Cognitive or mental rehabilitation for post-stroke patients involving speech and physical therapy as well as memory aids assist the brain's reorganization of the basic impaired functions.

When a patient relearns to carry out basic tasks, neurogenesis occurs. The goal is to stimulate the brain to reform lost pathways and circuits. And while it's true that brain cells can regenerate, they also can deteriorate if not being used. So when it comes to using your limbs or memory, the familiar phrase applies, "Unless you use it, you'll lose it." For instance, if you don't use your right arm, the corresponding part of your brain will deteriorate. "Mental practice" is the term given to rehearsing activities and movements in the mind and is known to facilitate peak performance in world-class athletes, as we at the Waitley organization have been engaged in for more than 55 years.

More recently, studies have shown that mental practice can also be used along with other cognitive treatments on stroke patients and by others, including our returning servicemen and women who've been severely injured in battle, using mental imagery to visualize motor movements, which stimulates neuroplasticity processes, improving motor functions, especially arm movement.

Thought Performance Enhancement

In 1980, I was appointed to serve on the United States Olympic Committee's Sports Medicine Council as Chairman of Psychology to assist in the performance enhancement of

American Olympians. My daughter, Deborah, and I became certified biofeedback technicians, mentored by Dr. Thomas Budzynski, an early pioneer in the field.

We began to participate in seminars and workshops using biofeedback instrumentation to demonstrate how our thoughts could impact brain and body functions. We used EEG (electroencephalograph) instruments to show how music and relaxation can produce different brainwave frequencies and moods. We employed EMGs (electromyographs) to measure muscle responses to certain thoughts. We used digital thermometers to show that warm thoughts could elevate temperatures in the blood flow in our extremities. And we used GSR (galvanic skin response) instruments to illustrate that words and images produce an immediate stress response on the surface of our skin.

We saw firsthand how the combination of an EEG and a GSR could detect the stress associated with untrue statements, that lie detectors have merit, and that spoken words and visual images repeated with emotional intensity have a definitive impact on our central nervous system.

I recall one Olympic hopeful expressing his amazement at what these biofeedback instruments could reveal. He said, "Wow, these machines do incredible things." And I responded with a smile, "These instruments are simply high-tech bathroom scales. They're just responding to you. You are controlling the outcomes internally."

Since those early days of neuropsychology, quantum leaps have been made in the brain-trained field. Neurofeedback has progressed well beyond the biofeedback clinics of the 1980s and '90s with sophisticated readouts that display how different parts of the brain are reacting to video images, sounds, colors, thoughts, and simulations.

By observing PET scans of people either watching or imagining various scenes, brain researchers know that the brain doesn't know the difference between real, watched, or imagined experiences. Neuropsychology today offers definitive proof that repeated vivid mental rehearsal over time can create an infrastructure in the brain that can convert virtual reality into reality.

> # There is definitive proof that repeated vivid mental rehearsal can convert virtual reality into reality.

New research has proven that our brains develop neural pathways from frequently used chemical messaging patterns and thus build synaptic connections that support habitual trains of thought. If I were to post this on X/ Twitter, all I would say is the brain train is on track to change your life. If you do it right in drill, you can get it right in life. Practice makes permanent, and the more perfect the practice, the more excellent the result.

"Lower"	"Higher"
Associated with survival, ego, and reactive thinking	Associated with awareness, integration, synthesis, and intuition
Limbic System: amygdala, hypothalamus & hippocampus—governs emotional reactivity, fear, reward-seeking, and basic memory **Basal Ganglia**: Habit formation, pattern recognition (good or bad) **Brainstem**: Instincts, fight-or-flight, survival	**Prefrontal Cortex**: responsible for executive function, long-term vision, impulse control & empathy **Anterior Cingulate Cortex**: governs emotional regulation and compassion **Default Mode Network**: supports self-refection, day-dreaming, future envisioning—activated in rest, meditation, and deep introspection
• Operates in habitual loops and fight-or-flight responses • Obsessed with control, certainty, protection, and prediction • Tends toward black-and-white, dualistic and reactive thinking	• Holds multiple perspectives at once • Capable of empathy, ethical reasoning, and symbolic insight • Sees from above—connecting past, present, and future with clarity • Feels more like receiving than reacting

In the chapters that follow, we discuss how you can:

- Train your brain to replace unhealthy, unproductive habits with healthy, productive habits.

- Enhance goal-setting methods to produce more successful outcomes.

- Use the brain's internal pharmacy to improve your overall health.

- Bounce back from setbacks.

- Build positive relationships and winning teams.

The Brain's Gatekeeper

The brain's gatekeeper. Radiating upward from your brain stem is a small network of cells about four inches in length called the reticular activating system. It's just about the size and shape of a quarter of an apple and is one of the most important parts of your brain to understand and utilize to reach your goals.

Reticular Activating System

The reticular core of the brain dominates your behavior patterns, which include your eating habits, exercise habits,

The Brain Train Revolution

and the way you choose to live your life. It is perfectly placed to monitor all of the nerves connecting the brain and the body, and it knows what's going on better than any other single part of the brain. It can override activity in the spinal cord. It regulates the signals from the eyes, ears, and other sense organs. And is clearly linked to the display and feelings of emotions.

The reticular activating system performs the unique function of filtering incoming stimuli such as sight, sound, and touch, and deciding what information is going to become part of your experience. It decides what's important information and what is to be ignored. For example, if you live along a busy street, the reticular activating system quickly allows you to tune out the sound of the cars rushing by so that you can sleep peacefully at night.

Once you've made a decision that a certain value, thought, feeling, sound, or picture is significant to you, your reticular activating system is alerted and it immediately transmits to your consciousness any information it receives regarding that item. So when you buy a new car, for example, it is this network that suddenly causes you to notice all the cars of the same make or even the same color on the highway.

The beautiful feature about the reticular activating system is that you can program it to be on the alert for success-related inputs. If it knows you're looking forward to another eventful day, it will get you right out of bed.

> # You can program your reticular activity system to be alert for success-related inputs.

If your reticular activity system knows that you're looking for values and qualities in other individuals, it will hone in on values and qualities. If you're seeking more financial rewards, it will be extremely sensitive to any financially oriented data that could help you. The reticular activating system explains accident-prone people as it conversely explains success-prone people. It explains why some people see a problem in every solution—and why others see a solution for every problem.

While the reticular activating system is a physical part of the brain, the corresponding self-image is an abstract part of the brain's consciousness, a function of the mind, and your self-image is the habit thermostat that sets the limits and the ceiling on your performance in your world. And that's the subject of the next chapter.

Reflect and Connect

Think of something in your life that you weren't particularly good at. You had to work hard to develop yourself, and you were finally able to gain proficiency, or even excel. (This could be anything from your childhood on up to your current age.):

1. How did your brain, mind, or thoughts help you in this endeavor?

2. Can you see how, over a period of time, you were able to create the neural pathways that enabled you to develop a new skill, habit, or personal characteristic?

3. What is your current belief and confidence in your mind's ability to create a better life for yourself, one thought, and then one habit, at a time?

Chapter 5

Reimagining Your Life

We're born without a sense of self. Our minds are like computers with almost unlimited creative capacity, plus the ability to adjust, store, and retrieve data during every moment of our lives. First through our senses during infancy, then through language and observation, we record visual, verbal, and sensory diaries of ourselves. This recorded self-concept or self-image—when nourished and cultivate—is a primary field where happiness and success grow and flourish.

Limitations

Limits are physical in that biological and other health factors, age and skills, do impose certain restrictions on performance. However, these limits for most of us will never be fully tested because of the limitations caused by our beliefs.

Limitations are psychological. Over time, we all learn to raise or lower our expectations of ourselves because of our experiences. Disappointments become solid barriers. Successes give us confidence; and as we get older, we don't simply move past these limitations that we've internalized. Some of them stay with us throughout our lives.

> # Success means moving past internalized limitations.

Winners are constantly seeking growth and high performance, and incrementally keep raising the bar on these invisible barriers. I recall when working with a world-class Olympic high jumper, preparing for the summer games. He could clear the high jump bar in practice and in competition at 7 feet, 5 inches, but no higher regardless of the technique or the practice.

He wasn't paying close attention one day and we raised the bar an inch to 7 feet, 6 inches. Thinking it was still at the lower setting, he cleared it. When I told him what he had done, he looked at me in disbelief, almost agitated.

"But I can't jump that high," he exclaimed.

"You just did," I smiled. "You just conquered your own four-minute mile barrier."

Just as Roger Bannister did so many years ago. Once Bannister proved that it was possible to run a mile in under four minutes on May 6, 1954, suddenly more and more track stars were able to do it, proving an important lesson—once you stop believing something is impossible, it becomes possible.

> # When you stop believing something is impossible, it becomes possible.

Many individuals don't understand and believe that they, to a large extent, can control their outcomes in life. They feel like thermometers, reflecting that they are who they are because of what's happening to them in relation to the outside world. A thermometer rises or falls to meet the external environment, and most self-images are greatly influenced by what the media and our role models bombard our senses with on a daily basis.

However, *we do have control of our current thoughts.* We can reset our self-image like an internal thermostat from loser to winner, from average performance to peak performance and expand our comfort zones over time. Each of us has a number of comfort zones that we've developed throughout our lives that dictate the amount of discomfort we're willing to suffer before making adjustments.

Moving Out of Comfort Zones

Reflect for a moment on just how many of your behaviors are set into motion when you move out of these comfort zones. Too much can motivate as strongly as too little. On the level of conscious thought, there are any number of examples:

- How much time we feel comfortable in spending with those around us,

- How much effort we feel comfortable in expending on our daily priorities at the office or at home,

- How much money we feel comfortable in spending on our lifestyles, as well as

- How much money we feel comfortable in earning.

Think about it. Our self-worth can profoundly impact our net worth. On a physiological level, there are an infinite number of feedback systems that kick into gear when we leave the comfort zone.

Much as a thermostat runs our home heating and cooling system, the body's hypothalamus, a tiny organ in the brain, senses body temperature. Venturing out on the hot side of the comfort zone, warm blood from the inner core of the body is diverted by the hypothalamus in a wondrous manner that closes certain blood vessels and opens others nearer the surface of the skin where excess heat can be radiated away. Of course, the action of the hypothalamus in activating the sweat glands to return you to the comfort zone is no surprise. But did you know why? When perspiration evaporates from the surface of the skin, heat is removed and sweating is a process that lowers body temperature.

Moisten a portion of your hand and then blow on it. As the moisture evaporates, the skin is cooled. Is your hypothalamus getting the signal that you're dropping into the colder area of the comfort zone? No problem. Blood nearer the surface of the body is shunted inward to the core to conserve heat and your muscles are set into rapid small contractions to generate yet more heat. You call it shivering and it happens unconsciously automatically.

Our self-image can definitely be compared to a type of thermostat, keeping us in a psychological comfort zone.

With a low self-image, many people's psychological thermostats are set correspondingly low. Not believing that they're capable of much or worth much, the low self-image individuals are comfortable with mediocrity and being spectators. When challenged to venture out on the high side or take a chance to change the status quo, they pull back. "I'm not capable of that. That's beyond my meager abilities. It's not worth the effort. Why bother?" This is negative self-talk. They have discovered that their imaginations serve as a life-governing device, that if their self-image can't possibly see themselves doing something or achieving something, they literally cannot do it.

Remember, it's not what you are that holds you back. It's what you *think* you are *not*.

Your set point for winning is arrived at over time based on your belief in yourself, your abilities, and your worth practiced on a daily basis. With a strong and healthy belief in yourself and what you're capable of, you can go out and survive the stress of day-to-day living and reach worthy goals.

When your self-image thermostat moves into the higher ranges, you believe you can handle pretty much whatever is thrown at you. Winners become comfortable with peak performance and they become uncomfortable with lower performance. However, we all have good and bad days, so it becomes important for you to respond effectively to setbacks.

If your efforts to win fall below your comfort zones, you may feedback to your self-image some positive reinforcement and self-talk. "Next time, I'll do better. I can do that. More knowledge, training, and better concentration will win me that prize."

Winners see the act of winning before it ever happens. They act like winners, imagining with words, pictures, and feelings the roles they want to play. When they make errors, miss, or lose, they view failure as corrective feedback to help them hit their target next time. They give themselves a preview of coming attractions, and their coming attractions are usually the rewards of success rather than the penalties of failure.

Seeing in Advance

What you set in your mind's eye is what you get. Creativity is seeing in advance an idea that can become a solution to a major problem or need, and holding on to that idea until it works or until a better idea is implemented. Creativity is holding on to your dreams even when others laugh at you. Creativity comes from having mentors and coaches who are interested in your success, coaches who listen unconditionally, who praise often and criticize constructively the behavior that's undesirable while not directly criticizing the individual. Creativity is having curious leaders who are open to new ideas and to better ways of doing things and who are not so set in their ways that they prejudice everything in advance.

Unimaginative and unproductive people say, "It may be possible, but it's too difficult." Creative individuals say, "It may be difficult, but it's always possible."

> **Understanding the secret power of the imagined experience is fundamental to understanding high-performance human achievement.**

When we look in the mirror, there are three reflections: (1) the child of our past, (2) the person we are today, and (3) the person we will become. With the right role models and the right inputs into our brain's software program, we can change the perceptions that have twisted and colored our image of who we really are. Understanding this secret of the power of the imagined experience is a fundamental key to understanding high-performance human achievement. Who you see is who you'll be.

Visualization, Internalization, Realization

Einstein believed that imagination is more important than knowledge, for knowledge is limited to all we now know and understand, while imagination embraces the entire world, and all there will ever be to know and understand.

I've been imagining and fantasizing all my life, which was a useful escape from an early childhood environment laced with financial strife, alcohol abuse, disharmony, and divorce. I remember saying my prayers at night after my mom and dad's shouting matches about his habits and low income, "God, guide me never to drink, smoke, or get married." My father left home when I was nine, and we kids felt somehow that we were part of the cause, because of the financial burden. My mother remained negative and bitter throughout her life. I recall only rare occasions when she offered any positive encouragement.

I had a recurring fantasy about age 12. I was standing in a tuxedo, in an ornate theater with beautiful chandeliers, bowing humbly before an enthusiastic audience, giving me a standing ovation for what I had said or portrayed. It was so vivid and real to me. My imaginary mom and dad were in the front row, smiling, clapping along with the others, and this gave me a feeling that I had finally earned their approval. This vision continued until I was a young adult.

I forgot about those daydreams until 40 years later when I experienced an amazing moment of déja vu. I was actually standing in Carnegie Hall in New York City, in a tuxedo, receiving a standing ovation for a lecture on the psychology of winning. And even though my parents were not there in person, I imagined them sitting in the front row, smiling.

As I was humbly acknowledging the audience's positive response, I found myself saying silently to my missing mom and dad, "Am I okay now? Am I a good boy? A worthy son?" Visualization or mental simulation is not a new concept. We all have fantasized and acted out our life scripts, virtual reality shows, or magnificent epic movies at some point in our lives.

I've been experiencing and researching many different examples of high-performance visualization since my early years as a Navy pilot in the 1950s, later with NASA astronauts in the 1960s, and then up close and personal as Chairman of Psychology on the US Olympic Committee's Sports Medicine Council, during the 1980s. Olympians train up to 1,200 days for a few moments of competition. Astronauts simulate until the profoundly unknown is perfectly known. The strangely unfamiliar becomes intimately familiar.

I remember my own combat training as a naval aviator. My throat tightened as two enemy interceptors appeared on my radar screen, knowing that a heat-seeking missile would be locked onto my tailpipe in seconds, I executed an aerobatic maneuver into heavy cloud cover, but I pulled too many Gs and lost control of the plane. With a bad case of vertigo, I was thrown from the cockpit by the centrifugal force of the uncontrollable spin. I fell for what seemed like an eternity—about four feet, from the flight simulator onto the hangar floor.

The simulator door had unlocked, and I had forgotten to fasten my seatbelt. The instructors doubled up in laughter. My peers joined with some choice remarks as I lay sprawled on the control room floor. Even worse were the stares of members of Congress and other VIPs who had come to observe Naval Air Pacific warriors display their superb combat skills. Being more like Will Ferrell than Tom Cruise was hard on my ego, but the fallout included an important leadership lesson.

"Just be glad this was a simulator," my instructor said, shrugging. "There are no second chances with the real thing."

> # Your mind can't distinguish between imagined and real experience.

What I learned that day, over 50 years ago, I later have confirmed again and again—*the mind can't distinguish between imagined and real experience.* The mind stores as truth everything vividly rehearsed in practice, which is why *it's so vital to store winning instead of losing images and correct your mistakes as they're made,* focusing on how to do it right next time. This is the centerpiece of our program.

Deborah~

As a young child I had dreamed of possibly becoming a singer like my mother. I dabbled in a few musical instruments, learned a few chords on the guitar, and joined the middle school and church choirs at my mother's urging, but I wasn't an exceptionally good singer and grew discouraged with thoughts that I would never be "good enough." Instead, I gravitated toward the field of human behavior and became interested in the inner workings of the mind and soul. I worked long and hard for a couple of decades to develop the knowledge and skills needed to build a stable career in this field, while supporting myself as a single mother. But the dream of my early childhood was buried and long forgotten.

I was well into my thirties and immersed in my PhD studies, when I came across an exercise for using your imagination and visualization. It was titled "Living Your Wildest Dream," and I decided to take on this challenge and give it my all. As instructed, I wrote these words at the top of a journal page and then unleashed my creative imagination.

Within a few minutes my mind soared to a huge arena with thousands of people applauding where I was performing and singing on a large stage. *It was dark all around me except for the colors of the stage lights and a beam of bright white light shining from above. I could make out the faces in the crowd, and our eyes met.* Ah yes, my wildest dream...

Returning to the reality of my open journal, I was prompted to write "Rock" and "Star." I laughed out loud and rolled my eyes as two additional words overrode the previous ones: "Yeah" and "Right." But something was awakened in me. This dream had made its way from the cellars of my subconscious to the light of my conscious mind, and was now made visible on the journal page. I was suddenly fueled with a newfound energy I felt compelled to act on immediately.

I signed up for vocal lessons and set aside time each day to practice vocal exercises and learn guitar chords. I was terrified of performing, but visualized myself poised and calm on an imaginary stage. I saved enough money to buy a guitar, and an acoustic performance amplifier (which enhanced the quality of my voice, thus boosting my confidence). Over the coming months, I began to feel like a real performer and pictured myself playing in public.

I battled constantly with my inner critic and the judgmental voices of *"You're too old," "This is crazy," "You can't start a music career this late in life," "You're not any good," "You have no experience,"* and so on. But every night before going to sleep, I wrote about my progress toward my dream.

Ten months later, on a whim, I answered an ad that read: "Wanted, back-up female vocalist with some guitar experience for adult rock/alternative band working on CD and live performance projects." Two weeks later, as a full-fledged member of "Diamond in the Rough," I was playing a live gig at a local coffeehouse. My dream reached its zenith another ten months later on the stage of an outdoor amphitheater to a sold-out summer crowd, opening for "Three Dog Night," one of my favorite bands back in middle school when I was singing in the choir.

In a synchronistic moment, I was lucidly aware of my surroundings: *It was dark all around me, except for the colors of the stage lights and a beam of white light that shone from above*—a full moon. *I could make out the faces in the crowd, and our eyes met.* They were part of my dream, which was now a reality. We later recorded a CD, performed at numerous venues, including Sea World and the Las Vegas strip.

> # Never underestimate the power of your dreams, and the fuel of your imagination–no matter how wild or seemingly impossible

The Mental Edge

My first interest in becoming involved in the Olympic movement began when I was working at the Salk Institute in La Jolla, California, about six years after leaving the Navy. I was always fascinated by the observation that at the world-class level in any endeavor, but especially in sports, that talent is nearly equal. The winning edge to me has always been the mental edge: mind over muscle, mind over environment, mind over circumstance.

My first live Olympic experience began in the late 1960s. The air was thin and still on that October afternoon in 1968, and there was a hush of anticipation in the Olympic stadium. Bob Beamon had just leaped nearly 30 feet in the long jump, a record that remains unbroken as of this writing. The attention of the 84,000 spectators at the Mexico City Olympics was now centered on the high jump bar, set at 2.24 meters, approximately 7 feet, 4.2 inches, a record height at the time.

The athlete was a carrot-top, freckle-faced youth by the name of Dick Fosbury, who had revolutionized the art of high jumping with the invention of a backward head-first dive, known as the Fosbury Flop. While the throng sat mutely, eyes glued to the bar awaiting Fosbury's attempt, it intently studied Fosbury's pre-jump concentration. He stood about 20 yards directly in front of the bar, preparing for a straight-ahead running approach. His eyes were closed, his hands opened and closed rhythmically at his sides, and he rocked back and forth, toe to heel.

This ritual continued for nearly eight minutes, and the crowd began to murmur softly becoming anxious. And the television commentator wondered aloud what was going on. Then with no warning, Fosbury broke into a lope that developed into a relaxed sprint. As he neared the bar, he rotated his body 180 degrees on the way up, arched his back in a reverse swan dive and cleared the bar, which didn't even tremble, for a new world record.

Even more amazing than the feat of winning was Fosbury's own revelation of how he did it. In an interview after the competition, we learned that Dick Fosbury, like so many other champions, was a master of visualization. As Fosbury rocked back and forth with eyes closed, he was mentally picturing every step to the bar, the push-off, the rotation, the back arch, the feet position in advance, and when the mental rehearsal gave him a vivid picture of his success in clearing the bar, it was his signal that he was ready.

I believe that I've learned more from Olympic coaches like Herb Brooks during the Miracle on Ice, Olympic Ice hockey victory in 1980, and Olympic champions like Mary Lou Retton and Carl Lewis in 1984, than they ever learned from me. And for the past 30 years, our institute has been able to document what we've observed in world-class athletes.

According to Michael Phelps, the most decorated Olympian of all time, his success stems from first visualizing each race before he even steps into the pool. Phelps says that he's been visualizing since he was seven years old, watching what he calls his video of the perfect swim in his mind each night before going to sleep, *mentally mapping out the ideal swim for the next day.*

Renowned Olympic gold medalist and World Cup skiing champion Lindsey Vonn says that her mental practice gives her a competitive advantage on the course. She says, "I always visualize the run before I do it. By the time I get to the start gate, I've run that race a hundred times already in my head, picturing how I'll take the turns." Not only does Lindsay pre-play visual images in her mind, she also simulates the path by shifting her weight back and forth as if she were on her skis, while practicing the specific breathing patterns that she'll use during the race.

When asked about athletic skills versus mental skills, Michael Jordan, one of the greatest NBA basketball players of all time, said, "The mental part is the hardest part, and I think that's the part that separates the good players from the great players." And using mental imagery, Jordan said, "I visualized where I wanted to be, what kind of player I wanted to become. *I knew exactly where I wanted to go, and I focused on getting there.*"

And one of my favorite Hall of Famers to be, NFL legendary quarterback Peyton Manning put it simply this way, "Some guys need to see things on a grease board. I like when you can see it in your mind."

In every sport, visualization is in the spotlight, whether it's Jack Nicklaus discussing going to the movies in his mind, pre-playing each shot before striking the golf ball. Or Carly Lloyd, member of the 2015 Women's World Cup Soccer Championship team and the first player to ever score three goals in a World Cup final, reflecting how she takes time before each game to visualize positive scenarios between herself and the soccer ball.

Visual Imagery and Mental Rehearsal

Visualization is not reserved for pilots, astronauts, and athletes only. Sales executives, scientists, surgeons, Navy SEALs, dancers, musicians, actors, parents, teachers, and students do it every day. Visualization can also be used to improve health and well-being, which we'll discuss in a later chapter. During the past decade, the techniques involved in visual imagery and mental rehearsal have grown from the oversimplified concepts of positive thinking, to more scientific approaches that incorporate high-speed cine-matography, digitized computer readouts, and stop-action video replay, neurofeedback techniques and simulation technology. Certain kinds of music, colors, images, and sensory environments can evoke different brainwave and emotional responses.

Virtual reality technology, which many people associate with video games, has many beneficial applications. Visualization works because the mind reacts automatically to the information we feed it in the form of words, pictures, and emotions. And as we have discussed, the brain's neural pathways can be reshaped and redirected.

Receptive and Programmed Visualization

Basically, there are two types of visualization: receptive and programmed.

Receptive visualization is used to help answer a question or find a solution to a problem. In this type of visualization, the question is formulated or the problem posed. First, the issue is analyzed logically for better understanding, and then a mental picture of a blank screen is formed and the answer or solution is allowed to appear on the screen in its own time. This technique is especially helpful in recalling information that appears to have been forgotten or lost.

Programmed visualization is used to get what we want in life. We picture what we want repeatedly and the brain sends signals to the body that cause us to take action to bring about the desired results. Make sure you really want what you're visualizing. Never picture a condition or event that you don't want to occur. The following are some specific tips for visualizing successfully.

First, when you visualize yourself doing something, make it an action scene in which there's movement. In sports psychology, this is referred to as VMBR, Visual Motor Behavior Rehearsal. And the object is to create a neurological pathway, enabling your muscles to remember the sequence of movements that make up an action. Therefore, no still pictures please.

Second, visualize both the successful outcome and the steps leading up to it. Olympic athletes mentally run through what they want to do and how they want to do it. Well before they arrive at the arena, they imagine the sights, sounds, temperatures, spectators, the other competitors, and then they focus on their own performances. Some even include a clock or stopwatch in their imagery, to ensure that the timing and pacing in their minds are exact. To your brain, a dress rehearsal is the opening night performance.

Third, visualize conditions and things that are consistent with your principles and moral values. If there's a conflict, you'll be less likely to get your mind and body working in concert.

Four, most importantly, when you visualize yourself, see yourself in the present as if you are already accomplishing your goal. Make certain that your visual image is as you would see it through your own eyes, not watching through the eyes of a spectator. If you're a skier, your imagery would appear in your mind as if an invisible TV camera were mounted on your shoulder, looking exactly where your eyes are focused during a ski run, and feeling the same sensations. If you need to give a speech, you should imagine exactly how the audience will look sitting in front of you.

Strengthen Your Visualization Capability

To strengthen your visualization capability:

- Start making mental notes about all the experiences that make up your life. Take in as many sights, sounds, smells, textures, and tastes as you can. Recreate in your mind the beauty of a sunrise or sunset. Feel the wet sand of a beach between your toes. As you become more curious, observant, and in tune with your surroundings, you'll find your powers of visualization improve greatly. And the more often you see the winner's circle in your mind's eye, the sooner you'll arrive there in person.

- Be more curious about everything around you. Use visual images more in your everyday conversation. As you listen to someone talk, try to form a mental image of the situation that he or she describes. Allow the words to form images, feelings, and sensations. By linking feelings and images, you'll be able to recall both better.

- When you talk to others, use words that are rich in visual imagery. Word pictures, analogies, stories, metaphors, and similes create vivid mental pictures and you'll enjoy a side benefit of becoming a better conversationalist and public speaker if you do.

Our minds have become lazy with so much incoming mental stimuli doing the work for us. Whether you are new to guided imagery or already an active visualizer, these skills and techniques are designed to stretch and strengthen the potential of your imagination. You'll expand the awareness of all your senses—sight, sound, smell, taste, and kinesthetic feel, as well as your emotional sensations—which ensure a much richer experience and greater success in creating lasting, positive change in your life.

Enhance Your Receptivity

We've used similar sessions with Olympians, professional athletes, business professionals, students, patients, and clients. In our follow-on training and coaching programs, you will hear research-based electroacoustic sounds in the background which are a unique blend of tones, frequencies, vibrations, and resonance, especially designed for our institute to enhance your receptivity and overall experience.

You can listen to these on your smartphone, tablet, or laptop, preferably with headphones to receive the full acoustic and experiential benefits. You will only need 10 minutes of your time for each session when you sit or lie down in a relaxed position. If you're in a car, park it; you should not be multitasking. When you are relaxed, you'll hear the voice of my daughter, Dr. Deborah Waitley, who has researched this entire program with me. She will guide you on your personal journey in creating a new pathway toward fulfillment.

Remember, what you see and what you feel will become real.

Deborah~

PREPLAYING THE FUTURE— PRACTICAL APPLICATIONS IN THE WORKPLACE

In my corporate consulting career, I've had many opportunities to facilitate strategic planning sessions and team-building workshops for Fortune 500 companies. On numerous occasions, visualization techniques have been effective tools in assisting companies, departments, teams, and individuals create powerful visions and missions for themselves for the coming year. Countless individuals were able to overcome specific weaknesses and improve their effectiveness, particularly in customer-facing interactions directly linked to revenue generating potential.

An exercise I use titled "PrePlaying Your Success," stands out as having a powerful impact on future outcomes. High-level consultants, for one of the "Big 4" international consulting firms, were given two days to plan and prepare for a hypothetical client presentation to retain a significant block of new business. Instead of the usual pages and pages of prepared data, along with complex graphs and charts on PowerPoint slides, they were told they could only use physical "props"—consisting of an array of art/craft items, or anything else they wanted to find—a whiteboard, and most importantly, themselves! They were to *become* the storyboard, the delivery mechanism for the presentation.

A key component in this preparation was the "Think, Feel, Say, and Do" exercise. The consultants met in small groups to brainstorm and imagine *how* they wanted the potential client to *respond during and after* their presentation. They were given a worksheet divided into four quadrants and asked to come up with a comprehensive list of desired outcomes:

- What will the client THINK?
- How will the client FEEL?
- What will the client SAY?
- What will the client DO?

When music is played during exercises, it helps the brain's Default Mode Network (DMN) activate when in a relaxed state. The DMN consists of and works with a number of regions and functions to facilitate creativity and abstract thinking. It supports divergent thinking, allowing for the imagining of novel images, and fostering of free-flowing, conceptual thinking. Music can help the DMN evoke memories or help envision future events such as rehearsing for a performance.

Watching the consultants deliver their "mock" client presentations at the end of the workshop was a phenomenal experience for all involved. Many of them were not strong in public speaking or client presentations, but the energy in the room as a result of their delivery could certainly be worth millions of future revenue!

Because they had pre-played the future results in their minds *while* they were creating their presentations, without realizing it, their brains were *already* anchoring, wiring, and locking in these successes before the actual event. Sounds like magic—but it's the reality of our brain "on fire" by imagining the possible!

Reflect and Connect

Recall a time in your life when you had a dream to achieve something that was really important to you.

1. If it, or any part of it became a reality, to what do you attribute your success?

2. How effective (and detailed) was your imagination in achieving a positive outcome?

3. What is a positive future outcome you can pre-play right now, to override a current fear or obstacle in your life?

Chapter 6

Reprogramming Your Software

First, let's review some key points we've covered so far:

- Self-esteem is how you feel about yourself.

- Self-image is how you see yourself.

- Self-confidence is proof of your value through your actions.

- Winners believe in their dreams when that's all they have to hang on to.

- Your mind stores as reality what you vividly, repeatedly imagine.

- What you visualize and internalize you can come to realize.

Studies conducted by a Stanford University research team reveal that what we watch has a major effect on our imaginations, our learning patterns, and our behaviors. First, we're exposed to new behaviors and characters. Next, we learn to acquire these new behaviors. The last and most crucial step is that we adopt these behaviors as our own.

> # Repeated viewing and repeated verbalizing shapes our future.

One of the most critical aspects of human development we need to understand is the influence of repeated viewing and repeated verbalizing in shaping our future. The information goes in harmlessly, almost unnoticed on a daily basis, but we don't react to it until later when we aren't able to realize the basis for our reactions. In other words, our values are being formed without any conscious awareness on our part of what is happening.

Modeling is a potent learning tool that goes far beyond simple imitation. Imitation or simulation is a conscious training process by which a person intentionally copies the behavior of someone else. Modeling takes place unconsciously, as one individual gradually assumes the characteristics of someone else, particularly someone who he or she likes or admires. *The capability of your mind to pre-play and replay performances as if they were really happening is the central theme in resetting your self-image.*

Engrave Your Mind

Current neurological and psychological research confirms the incredible ability of the mind to drive the body to achieve the person's immediate dominant thought by instructing the body to carry out the vivid images of performance, as if they had been achieved before and are merely being repeated. With pre-play simulation or feed-forward, you can engrave in your mind the verbal, visual, and emotional conditions associated with high performance, good health, and long life. This process greatly influences your daily habit patterns and acts as a steering program toward your goals. With replay simulation or feedback, you can replay your successes during quiet times or on off days to reinforce your self-confidence in stressful times.

Feedback also allows you to enter new positive corrective data into your thoughts so you can reset your aim on goals that were previously missed. It's interesting to observe that children don't learn how to pre-play failure until their parents, peers, and other role models repeatedly show them how. And also, it's sad to see children and adults who've been taught to dwell on past mistakes, instead of using them as learning experiences to reinforce their blessings and accomplishments. *When your mind talks, your body listens and acts accordingly.*

Research has shown that our thoughts can raise and lower body temperature, secrete hormones, relax muscles and nerve endings, dilate and restrict arteries, and raise and lower pulse rate. With this evidence, it's obvious that we need to control the language we use on ourselves. Winners rarely talk negatively about themselves before or after a performance. They use positive self-talk and positive feedback self-talk as part of their training programs until it becomes a force of habit. They say, "I can, I will. Next time I'll get it right. I'm feeling better. I'm ready. Thank you."

Losers, on the other hand, fall into the trap of saying, "I can't. I'm a klutz. I can't stay in shape. I wish. If only. I should have. Yeah, but."

You are your most important critic. There is no opinion as vitally important to your success, fitness, and well-being as the opinion you have of yourself. The most important meetings, briefings, coaching sessions, and conversations you'll ever have are the conversations you have with yourself.

As you read this, you're talking to yourself. Let's see if I understand what is mean by that. How does that compare with my own experiences? I already knew that. I think I'll try that.

Andre Agassi, former world number-one tennis player and eight-time Grand Slam champion, has related how mental practice before a match has helped him throughout his career. Tennis is one of the most solitary of all sports where the player is alone in his or her head without the benefit of a coach, caddy, or corner man for an average of three and one-half hours. Agassi reports to using a 22-minute afternoon shower to work on his self-talk, saying things to himself over and over until he believes them. In Agassi's best-selling autobiography, Open, he cites how important his shower routine was in winning matches, writing, "I've won 869 matches in my career, fifth on the all-time list, and many were won during the afternoon shower."

We believe that this self-talk, this psycholinguistics or language of the mind, is critical to our success and can be controlled to work for us in achieving our goals of health, performance, and longevity. We're all talking to ourselves every moment of our lives, except during certain portions of our sleeping cycle, it comes automatically. We're seldom even aware that we're doing it. We all have a running commentary going on in our heads on events and on our reactions to them.

Since most of the negative kinds of feelings, beliefs, and attitudes that we have about ourselves are stored through habitual repetition, we need to start relaxing and using self-talk that is constructive and complimentary, instead of destructive and derogatory.

Don't let the technique of positive self-talk give you the false impression that you're brainwashing or kidding yourself. On the contrary, we are suggesting just the opposite. You are unconsciously being brainwashed by the television shows and movies you watch, by the lyrics you listen to, and by the people you talk to. All of these give you a sensationalized perception of what is happening in the world. Much of what you see and hear is negative because bad news attracts more attention and sells better.

Isn't it time you concentrate on information desired for your success rather than your distress? There is little difference between champions and the rest of the pack. The little difference is attitude and the big difference is whether your attitude is positive or negative. When you talk to yourself, talk yourself up.

Scripting Self-Talk

In our previous research with astronauts, executives, and other individuals functioning under pressure and in our continuing observation of Olympic athletes and high achievers in virtually every profession throughout the world, there's a technique of scripting self-talk that seems to be the most effective. The Olympic athletes call this technique the "self-statement" or "image of achievement." Psychologists and psychiatrists call it "cognitive reconstruction" or "the practice of reframing by internalizing positive thoughts."

There are three basic types of self-statements:

One, general self-talk.

These are affirmative statements that can be used at any time and place for a feeling of general well-being. Some examples, "I like myself. I'm glad I'm me. I'm relaxing now. I'm at peace. I'm in control of my body. I feel that my body is more healthy now. I give the best of me in everything. I am strong and full of energy. I respect and appreciate myself. I'm a winner."

Two, specific self-talk.

These statements are used to project and reframe as well as reaffirm our specific skills, goals, and attributes. Some examples, "I'm a team player. I create value in everything I do." For a woman, it could be "I weigh 125 pounds and feel trim in my bathing suit." For a man it might be, "I feel healthy at my best weight of 175." Overall we can say, "I drink a glass of water with every meal. I arrive for appointments on time. I am calm and confident when I take an exam. I appreciate others' opinions. I eat fish or poultry to get my lean protein. I speak with authority in front of a group."

Three, process self-talk.

These are one-word or two-word self-statements that can be used as trigger ideas at mealtime, during an exercise workout, or during the performance of professional sporting or other demanding skills. Some examples, "Concentrate, focus, backhand follow-through, easy, push-off, relax, let's go." Your process-specific self-talk. Before a performance, pre-play a positive self-image about specific activities in your life. Your performance will improve because of your elevated self-image, and sometimes your performance will exceed your expectations. So then your feedback self-talk will say, "Good for me. Now we're getting somewhere." On occasion, your performance will fall short of your expectations. Your feedback self-talk will say, "Next time I'll do better. I'll make a target correction to get it right."

A Secret to Success

One of the secrets of success is that our responses to our performances in words, images, and feelings are just as important as our self-images or simulations of ourselves before we ever attempt to perform in the first place. The vicious cycle is created by negative anticipation and a negative response to what happens in your daily life. The victor's circle is created by positive anticipation to what's going to happen in your daily life, and a positive reaction no matter what happens. It's not what happens that means the most. It's how you take it and what you make of it so that next time it will be better.

> # The victor's circle is created by positive anticipation to what's going to happen in your daily life, and a positive reaction no matter what happens.

In order for these self-statements to be most effective, it's extremely important to construct and phrase them properly. The following are specific guidelines for you to use in developing self-talk skills to strengthen your eating habits, your exercise habits, and your professional and personal lifestyle habits:

- Decide to turn negative self-talk into positive affirmations.

- Listen to what you're saying and thinking in anticipation of and in response to your daily challenges.

- Become aware of your own negative self-talk and construct affirmative self-talk statements to replace the negativity.

- Use positive explanatory statements concerning your professional and personal goals, health, and daily experiences. Pessimists rarely inspire themselves or others to win.

- *Respond* rather than react to the negative self-talk of others.

The next time someone offers you some of his or her negative statements, don't agree mentally. You can learn either to ignore the comment and say nothing, or turn it around and help that person with your positive response to the comment. Direct your self-talk toward what you desire instead of what you're trying to come away from that you don't want. Your mind can concentrate on the reverse of an idea. If you try to tell yourself not to repeat mistakes, your mind will reinforce the mistake. You want to *focus your current dominant thought on your desires, not your dislikes.* This is critically important.

Consider the following effective and ineffective self-talk:

Effective: "I arrive early for appointments. I am patient and loving with my children." Always use personal pronouns such as I, my, and me, which personalizes your statements and makes them easier to internalize. "I'm in control of my habits. I weigh a slim trim 125 pounds." Or for a man, "I feel healthy at 175."

Ineffective: "Jogging is good exercise. Smoking isn't good for me. I'm too fat and have to lose weight. I won't be late anymore. I won't yell at the kids."

Effective: "I enjoy jogging three times a week." Keep your self-talk in the present tense. Referring to the past or future may be counterproductive in making progress.

Ineffective: "Someday I'll get in good physical condition."

Effective: "I look forward to the next sale."

Ineffective: "I won't lose those sales again."

Effective: "I gain and retain loyal customers." Keep your self-talk non-competitive instead of measuring yourself against others.

Ineffective: "I will beat John out of the next starting position."

Effective: "I am starting on the team and doing the job well." In writing your statements, concentrate on incremental improvement over your previous performance. Don't strive for perfection or unrealistic superhuman efforts.

Ineffective: "I am the club champion every year."

Effective: "The more I practice the right swing, the better I get."

Once you have correctly constructed images of achievement in the form of self-statements for your goals, write these statements in a journal or smartphone or record them in your own voice on a laptop, tablet, or handheld device. Read or listen to the statements at the beginning of your normal routine. Get to know them during the day, and review them again before you retire at night.

Visualize yourself as having already reached each goal that you're simulating. Allow yourself to actually feel the pride in doing well. You should be your own coach, mentor, and best friend since you spend more time with you than with anyone else.

And remember, you'll be training your brain into new pathways toward high achievement and fulfillment.

Reflect and Connect

Research has shown that approximately 77% - 80% of the thoughts we think each day are negative. Surprisingly, 95% of these are the same repetitive negative thoughts as the day before.

1. What is an estimation of your current ratio of negative to positive thoughts and self-talk?

2. How often does your mind automatically "default" to a potential negative outcome?

3. How quickly are you able to "catch yourself" using negative self-talk?

4. What overall positive self-talk statement could you incorporate right now to help ensure your dialogue stays positive throughout the day?

Chapter 7

Your Internal GPS: Goal Positioning System

No one really has a time management problem. We really have a focus problem. We spend too much energy worrying about the things we want to do, but can't, instead of concentrating on doing the things we can do, but don't.

Dreams are the creative vision of our lives in the future. Dreams are what we would like our lives to become. Goals, on the other hand, are the specific events that we intend to make happen. Goals should be just beyond our present reach, but never out of sight. Think of your goals as previews of coming attractions of an epic real-life movie in which you are the screenwriter, producer, and star performer. Goals are our method of concentrating energy.

By defining what needs to be done within reasonable time limits, we have a way of measuring success. Concentrate your attention on where you want to go, not away from where you don't want to be.

> # Goals should be just beyond our present reach, but never out of sight.

You will always move in the direction of your currently dominant thoughts, so think of your mind as a marvelous GPS system. But instead of global positioning satellite system, either handheld or in our cars, your brain is like a GPS system, where GPS means **G**oal **P**ositioning **S**ystem. Tell your internal GPS where you want to go. Be as specific as possible. The more inputs, the better. And it will guide you there.

But first, you must know where you are right now and where you want to go. You are the world's greatest expert on yourself. No one knows more about your hopes, your dreams, your fears, and frustrations than you do. In your secret heart, your goals are quite clearly defined, and most likely, they have been since your childhood. That doesn't mean, however, that you won't choose to delude yourself about them. All of us feel the pressure of what we believe the world expects us to do and be. And under that pressure, most of us feel the need to compromise on what we really want from life.

This is part of growing up, and it's inevitable. But the danger arises when we convince ourselves that growing up means not just adjusting but abandoning what we really want and need. And this happens because we spend too much time fantasizing and not enough time prioritizing and internalizing.

Some people believe the law of attraction means throwing a dream out into the universe and expecting the universe to respond like the genie in Aladdin's magic lamp. I believe the law of attraction takes daily action. Today is a new starting point for your journey. Ask yourself, "If there were no constraints of money, time, or circumstance, what would I begin doing tomorrow?"

To answer this important question, use these other key questions as guidelines on your GPS screen in your mind:

- What did you love to do as a child?

- Are you doing what you enjoy now in your personal and professional life and using your talents fully?

The Neuro-Psychology of Winning

- Are you making a contribution to the world and to other people, that gives you a feeling of self-respect?

Even if you're not pursuing your childhood aspirations today, it's still important to think back to what you love to do and what talents you displayed at an early age. Remember to identify your personal character strengths, your natural abilities, and educational experiences that may have brought you special knowledge and skills. Make note of the people who are your primary personal network of role models and mentors, who I refer to as sounding boards and springboards on the road to success.

Back to the Future

By journaling these in writing, you can create a detailed self-assessment of where you are today, in relation to your goals. You can give real meaning to the phrase, "Back to the future." If you don't take a practical approach to achieving your goals, sooner or later, you'll start beating yourself up for your pie-in-the-sky dreams and you'll start settling for less than you really want—because you don't clearly see how anything more is possible.

While I was a naval officer in Washington, DC, after the Korean War, I conducted a study of North Korean and Chinese interrogation methods. These methods were designed to separate and identify any captured Americans who could be turned into collaborators or informers. I discovered that it had been relatively easy for the captors to separate strong-willed leaders among their prisoners, from purposeless followers.

The interrogation appeared simple and nonthreatening: "Where are you from? Do you have a girlfriend back home? What are you fighting for? What are you going to do when you return home? What kind of career would you like most? What are you planning to study? How much money do you need? What is your favorite sports team? What is your religion?" Soldiers and airmen who gave specific, practical answers were classified as goal-oriented, potential leaders. They were placed in maximum security camps, were deprived of adequate food and shelter, and were tortured in an attempt to break their resolve.

But Americans who gave vague answers about their lives and their futures were recognized as ideal subjects for indoctrination, referred to as brainwashing. They were put in minimum security camps that were almost like country clubs, with no machine gun towers, no barbed-wire fences, and no guard dogs. Instead, there were comfortable barracks, cafeterias, and recreation areas.

Most importantly, there were study halls for reading and listening to communist propaganda.

Though the prisoners in the max security camps were beaten, starved, and forced to live in cages like animals, some escaped and got back to friendly territory. In contrast, no one escaped or even attempted to escape from the minimum security country clubs. And yet, incredibly, despite superior food, shelter, clothing, and medical care, death and disease rates were many times higher than in the maximum security camps. Having no tangible goals to motivate them in the minimum security camps, several of our young servicemen pulled the covers up over their heads and died, for no apparent reason, other than the absence of a cause for which to live.

If you don't know where you're going, it doesn't make any difference if the alarm clock goes off in the morning. If you don't stand for something, you'll fall for anything. But if your goals are vivid, specific, flexible, and supported by action plans and subgoals, you'll believe that your life is worth living and you'll be right.

> # ...the absence of a cause for which to live.

One of the major reasons so few people reach their goals is that most people don't set specific goals, and the mind just dismisses them as irrelevant. Most people want financial security, but have never considered how much money it will take. The mind cannot begin to formulate the strategies and actions required, without specific information. Your mind will simply not respond to a request to get rich, have more, do better, or make money. You must act like a bank loan officer with your goals. The reason loan officers want to see a detailed business plan in writing is because they know that entrepreneurs who are precise and specific are the ones who will succeed and pay off their loans.

> **Your mind cannot begin to formulate the strategies and actions required, without specific information.**

Specific Goals

Written goals are like contracts with yourself. *What you see is who you'll be and what you set is what you'll get.* In one of our early seminars, we divided 200 participants into groups of six attendees each, and they sat at circular tables. They wrote down and discussed their personal responses to each part in a series of five questions. The questions we asked were these:

1. What are your greatest personal and professional abilities and liabilities?

2. What are your most important personal and professional goals for the balance of this year?

3. What is a major personal and professional goal that you have for next year?

4. What will your professional level and annual income be in five years?

5. Twenty years from now, where will you be living? What will you be doing? What will you have accomplished that could be written or said about you by family or peers? What state of health will you enjoy? And what will your assets be in dollars?

Your Internal GPS: Goal Positioning System

They struggled trying to be specific, because most of them had work priorities or quotas assigned in their jobs, but had never given any definition or priority to their own personal goals. All but one person who was too young to have given up on his dreams. He was a red-haired, freckle-faced 10-year-old named Eric who tagged along with his father to get some positive input. Instead, his output startled the adults in the group.

When asked the five specific questions, he eagerly went down the list. He said his greatest talents were building model airplanes and doing well in computer games. He said he needed improvement in cleaning his room and being nice to his sister. His personal goal for that year was to build a model of the space shuttle, and his professional goal was to earn $400 doing yard work for neighbors.

For the following year, his personal goal was to take a trip to Hawaii, and his professional goal was to earn $700 for the Super Saver Travel Package. When asked about his five-year goals, he said, "I'll be 15 in the 10th grade, and I'll be taking a lot of math, science, and computer classes." Eric had to think for a moment when asked about his 20-year life goals. He said, "Twenty years from now, I'll be thirty years old, right? I'll be living in Cape Kennedy, Florida, as a space shuttle astronaut working for NASA. I'll be in great physical shape. You have to be in good shape and study hard to be an astronaut," he finished proudly.

"Just boyhood fantasies," you might think. Eric actually graduated from the Air Force Academy, entered flight training, and on his 31st birthday, he celebrated in outer space, aboard the space shuttle, putting a communications satellite into orbit.

How you frame your goals in your mind is very important, since your goals are images of achievement. We all know that every invention and product was first a thought, a figment of some creative individual's imagination.

Five Powers

The following are five powers that will help you create more focused goals to achieve your dreams.

1. The power of the positive.

Your goal should be framed in positive terms. Winners dwell on the rewards of success, while losers dwell on the penalties of failure. In other words, instead of focusing on not being late, not being fat, not being in debt, or not working in your regular job—you want to instead concentrate on images of achievement such as, "I'm an on-time person. I am lean and I'm in great shape. I'm financially free. And I'm creating wealth and success in my business." Remember that your mind cannot concentrate on the reverse of an idea, so keep your goals framed in the positive.

2. The power of the present.

Your goal should be framed as images of achievement in the present tense, as you affirm them in your own self-talk. Your long-term memory stores information in real time that is critically important to you. The reason that your memory stores information in the present tense is obvious. Can you imagine what would happen if your mind had to remind your heart to beat tomorrow? Or what if you put the command for breathing, eating, or calorie burning on next month's agenda? If you say, "I want to weigh a certain weight by next summer," your long-term memory won't consider working on this goal, because it's so far away. It will simply dismiss it as something that might come up later in the distant future. So by combining the first two powers, you'll have your goals framed in the present and in the positive. Some examples, "I weigh a lean, trim, healthy weight." Or you can make it an income image, such as, "My business is generating $150,000," or whatever the target is for this year.

3. The power of the personal.

Your images of achievement must be yours. They cannot be your boss's goals, your spouse's goals, or your friend's goals. They also cannot be goals that the media or film-makers are placing in front of you. Goals that are created by others for you have very little staying power. No goals set for you by others will ever be sought with the same passion, effort, commitment, or motivation as the one that you set for yourself. As you set your goals, share them only with those individuals who will take the time to give you positive feedback and input. Never share a personal image of achievement with a cynic, a jealous relative, or an acquaintance who is likely to rain on your parade. Share your goals only with winners who have similar goals, who have achieved similar goals, or who really are interested in helping you accomplish your own.

4. The power of precision.

Make your images of achievement specific and precise. Remember, when you talk about your goals and generalities, you will very rarely succeed. But when you talk about your goals with specificity, you will rarely fail. A good way for you to determine if your images of achievement are focused enough is to simply ask yourself, "Can this goal be timed, checked, or measured?" If you cannot time, check, or measure your performance, your goals are not specific enough.

5. The power of the possible.

A formula that works well is that your goals should be just out of reach, but not out of sight. Another way to state that—your goals should be realistic, but not achievable by ordinary means. You don't want the daydreaming pie-in-the-sky kind of goal—your goals must be challenging. So you can't get a loan for a goal or put it on a charge card. The challenge is what engages your mind to get the adrenaline flowing. Your goal should also be broken down into small, incremental action steps. Remember, the best way to eat an elephant is one bite at a time. So set challenging realistic goals, with small, doable action steps. The mind is the most magnificent biocomputer ever created, but remember, like a computer, it only responds to specific instructions, not vague ideas. Get specific in your goal mind, and you will soon have a gold mine of achievement.

Reflect and Connect

If we lose sight of any of our "5 Powers" for achieving our goals, we can soon find ourselves derailed from our track, becoming easily distracted or more susceptible to obstacles along the way.

1. What typically gets in your way of achieving your goals?

2. Are your obstacles more external or internal?

   If "external," review the questions at the end of Chapter 3, and determine what is in your power to control, specifically your thoughts and feelings.

3. In which of the 5 Powers do you need the most improvement? What can you do to further develop these?

4. In which of the 5 Powers are you strong? How can you build on these strengths to take your goal achievement to the next level?

Chapter 8

Habits: Our Invisible Robots

I love the challenge of trying to explain complex scientific theory and evidence in easy-to-understand ways. Years ago while relaxing at home, sharing mutual experiences with my family, sometimes person to person and sometimes as a group, I made the analogy about the self-image and R2-D2, the little robot of *Star Wars* fame. In the first *Star Wars* movies, R2-D2 had as his primary goal the hologram 3D projection of a video pre-recorded inside him. No matter what happened out in the galaxy, he was driven by his internal guidance system to complete his mission. I told my kids that each of them had their own droid or robot in their brains named R-U-Me-Too, the voice inside who tells you whether or not you really can or should do something.

A fantasy poem from my book, *The Psychology of Winning*, illustrates the point:

I have a little robot that goes around with me.

I tell it what I'm thinking, I tell it what I see.

I tell my little robot all my hopes and fears.

It listens and remembers all my joys and tears.

At first, my little robot followed my command,

But after years of training, it's gotten out of hand.

It doesn't care what's right or wrong or what is false or true.

No matter what I try, now it tells me what to do.

During every moment of our lives, we program—or we allow others to program—our brains to work for us or against us. Since our invisible automatic pilot has no judging functions, it strives to meet the attitudes and beliefs that we set for it, regardless of whether they're positive or negative, true or false, right or wrong, safe or dangerous. Its only function is to follow our previous instructions implicitly, like a personal computer playing back what is stored, responding automatically.

After *Star Wars* episode VII the Force Awakens hit the movie theaters, my grandchildren suggested that the R2-D2 analogy was old stuff, and that I should talk about programming the lovable droid BB-8 with our own map and dreams for the future. I told them I had used the R2-D2 metaphor on my audio tapes, and they looked puzzled and asked, "What are audio tapes?"

I changed the subject and agreed that the reference to BB-8 would be much more appropriate in my live-streaming and MP3 downloads on their smartphones. After all, some *Star Wars* fans have even put BB-8 tattoos on various parts of their bodies. We're simply hoping that you, the reader, will embed positive images and data in your brain.

Practice Makes Permanent

Many people have defined self-discipline as sacrificing or doing without—but a better definition of *self-discipline is doing within while you're doing without.* Self-discipline is no more than mental practice, the commitment to memory the thoughts, emotions, and daily actions that will override current information stored in the subconscious memory bank. Then, through relentless repetition, the penetration of these new inputs into our subconscious results in the creation of a new self-image.

We learn by observation, imitation, and repetition. First, we observe the behaviors of relatives, friends, or role models, then we imitate that behavior. Then when we repeat and internalize the behavior and the idea, the notion and act, belief grows layer upon layer from a flimsy cobweb into an unbreakable cable to strengthen or shackle our lives.

> # Bad habits are like comfortable beds, they're easy to fall into, but hard to get out of.

Unfortunately, bad habits take no holidays. There's no, "Thank goodness, it's Friday," for these mindless routines. Instead, like comfortable beds, they're easy to fall into, but hard to get out of. We repeat behavior until it is internalized, like brushing our teeth or driving our cars.

Think of your brain as a complex series of highways, overpasses, and side streets. When you drive to and from work or from your home to the store, you take the same route over and over again. It becomes second nature. The recent breakthroughs in neuroscience have shown that you can build new freeways and shortcuts in your brain to take you to new destinations that you may never have considered before. The unfamiliar becomes familiar, the roadblocks become overpasses and the dead ends become freeways.

Do you recognize this autobiography?

> You may know me. I'm your constant companion. I'm your greatest helper. I'm your heaviest burden. I'll push you onward or drag you down

to failure. I'm in your command. Half the tasks you might do might as well be turned over to me. I'm able to do them quickly and I'm able to do them the same every time, if that's what you want. I'm easily managed, all you have to do is be firm with me. Show me exactly how you want it done, and after a few lessons, I'll do it automatically.

I'm the servant of all great men and women, and of course, the servant of all the failures as well. I've made all the great winners who've ever been great, and I've made all the losers, too. But I work with the precision of a marvelous computer with the intelligence of a human being. You may run me for profit or you may run me to ruin. It makes no difference to me. Take me, be easy with me, and I'll destroy you. Be firm with me, and I'll put the world at your feet.

Who am I? I'm habit.

The Force of Habit

The force of habit is your greatest tool for success. We all first make our habits and then our habits make us, and it happens so subtly over time, imperceptibly, quietly beneath the notice of anyone. Habits are like submarines, they run silent and deep. The chains of our habits are usually too small to be recognized until they're too strong to be broken. When we allow unhealthy habits to be our guide and counsel, we give up control of our actions and find ourselves at the mercy of that blind giant who calls the shots without any concern for our well-being.

However, when we begin to deal with the attitudes and actions that bind us, we give ourselves permission to take control and to build new habit patterns that help us perform to our ultimate potential. There's a critical difference between knowing something and learning how to make it a part of our everyday game plan. The secret is repetition, repetition, repetition. Repetition creates habit, habit becomes conviction, conviction controls action.

Right now in this instant, you're engaged in one of the best habits of all, that of experiencing information that will benefit you, rather than frustrate and defeat you. Advertising executives on Madison Avenue bet their entire careers and their clients' enormous budgets on the fact that repeated messages cause subconscious decisions. Every Saturday morning, they teach our kids which brands of cereal they should eat, what kind of shoes are cool, and which video games, cell phones, software, and toys they should get their parents to buy.

While our brains receive thousands of inputs each day, it seems that we lock in most aggressively on those that are negative. But the good news is you can change your life by changing your mindsets and, over time, create new habits.

> # You can change your life by changing your mindset and, over time, create new habits.

Psychologists have done scores of scientifically validated studies to find how habits are formed. We now know how to track a habit from the time the sensory nerves carry the message from our hearing, touch, vision, taste, and smell to the data processing areas of our brains. The brain then makes the decision, based on this information, and immediately sends the work order through the motor nerves to the appropriate parts of the body, demanding action.

Habit Forming

It should then come as no surprise that after the body responds the same way to identical stimuli a number of times, a habit is being formed. And here's the most interesting part. Because of this repetition, the message from the sensory nerve learns to jump over to the conditioned motor nerve without a conscious decision by the brain. Think about it, reframing your thoughts and actions repeatedly, and layer upon layer, new neural pathways are formed, which can be likened to new software programs installed in the hard drive of our computers. We don't think about it, we just run the program.

While it seems more difficult to replace a bad habit with a good one, the development of good habits enjoys the same sequencing. It depends on input, practice, and supporting environment. For a habit to become a permanent part of your life, it can take about a year of committed practice to firmly internalize it, and possibly longer for it to override your past experiences and former habits that have been developed over a lifetime. We're all wired differently, with each individual's physiology unique to that person; and therefore, timeframes for successful habit chains vary from being ingrained after two months to nearly a year of continual daily activity.

Four Cornerstones of Change

There are four ideas that we call the four cornerstones of change. Understanding these four concepts will help you understand the right way to develop healthy habits.

Cornerstone One

No one else can change you. You must first admit the need for change, give up any denial of your role in the problem, and take full responsibility for changing yourself. You must also understand that you can't change anyone else, either. You can influence and inspire others as a mentor, but they, as individuals, are ultimately responsible for gaining new inputs, practicing them, and surrounding themselves with a team of positive supporters.

Cornerstone Two

Habits are not easily broken, they're replaced by layering new behavior patterns on top of the old ones over time. Since many habits have been internalized for years, it's foolish to assume that three or four weeks of training will override the old destructive patterns. To change any habit, including substance abuse, self-ridicule, eating disorders, and any other destructive lifestyles, forget about the 30-day wonder cures, the 60-day diet delights, and the get-fit-get-rich-quick fads. Give yourself about a year to internalize permanent change. Be patient. It took a number of years of observation, imitation, and repetition for you to pick up and store your current habits.

Cornerstone Three

A daily routine adhered to over time will become second nature, like brushing your teeth or driving your car. Continue to practice your mistakes on the golf driving range and you'll remain a high handicap duffer. Learn from a professional and then practice the correct swing with each club as demonstrated by the pro, and you'll become the pride of your foursome.

Cornerstone Four

Once you change a habit, stay away from the old, destructive environment. The reason most criminals return to prison is that they make the mistake of returning to their old neighborhoods and their old friends when they're paroled the first time. No matter how much they regretted their actions while in prison and want to go straight, they're easily dragged back into their old ways by exposure to the negative environment. When dieters reach their desired weight, they usually go back to their former eating routines because their new behavior patterns haven't been embedded long enough to make them strong enough to pass by the dessert section of the buffet. Overweight individuals and dieters should stay away from the buffet lines. Think of where you want to be and you'll move toward that thought.

Before a marketing presentation, one successful businessman we know practices in his mind what he'll say and how he'll say it. He imagines what some of the obstacles will be. He focuses on the possible objections and questions his clients may have, and he rehearses how he'll overcome them. He sees himself being relaxed, confident, and in good humor. He sees the client satisfied in advance. Now he may have preferred to go to the sports bar the night before his presentation, but no, he practices self-discipline by staying home to spend a quiet evening rehearsing the day to come. If you do it right in drill, you will do it right in life. Practice makes permanent.

> **Think of where you want to be and you'll move toward that thought.**

Explain, Demonstrate, Correct, Repeat, Affirm

The greatest coaches of the greatest teams, the greatest parents of the greatest kids, and the greatest leaders of the greatest companies and countries use the same basic techniques: explanation, demonstration, correction, repetition, and affirmation. Remember, the idea is to replace habits, not try to erase them. You can't always practice in person on the field, in the office, with a client, or before the boss, but you can rehearse in your mind—and when your mind talks, your body does listen.

> # When your mind talks, your body listens.

The following are some action ideas you can use to reinforce the victor's circle in your professional and personal life:

- If you fail the first time, try again.

- If you fail the second time, get more feedback as to why you failed.

- And if you fail the third time, your sights may be too high for now, so bring your goals in just a little bit from the horizon.

- To remain optimistic and successful, avoid pity parties, group crappers, negative social media ranters, and internet chat groups of pessimists and quick-fix pushers.

Habits: Our Invisible Robots

- Network with people with similar goals and those who already are succeeding.

- You deserve as much happiness and success as anyone.

- You're worth the price, which is knowledge, attitude, skills, and habit training.

- You control your thoughts and your thoughts control your habits.

- Always remember that practice makes permanent.

- Your mind can't distinguish a vividly repeated simulation from a real experience. It stores as fact whatever you rehearse. The software drives the hardware, which is true for losers and winners.

- All pursuits begin with an idea of what is to be accomplished or attained.

- An image of achievement is a tool that permits us to provide accurately encoded information to the brain so that our mind can work with that information and can begin sharpening perceptions and marshaling resources toward the imagined goal.

- What we need most in life is continuing support and reinforcement of other winners with similar goals. Every week, meet before work, after work, or during lunch with one or more role models.

- Form a network with other success-conscious associates in your local community.

- In everything you do, think, speak, act, behave, and get the habit of success by association. Your mind and body can't distinguish rehearsal from the main event. It stores as reality whatever you practice. You become what you are most exposed to.

- Constantly expose yourself to successful individuals whose personal habits match their professional accomplishments. This is one of the most important concepts to learn and implement.

Reflect and Connect

How you begin each day—from the moment you open your eyes, think your first thoughts, and physically arise from your bed—can set the stage and determine the course your day takes. Think of an old habit you would like to break and identify a new positive habit that will take its place.

You can start carving out a new neuropathway in support of your new habit by adding something different to your morning routine. Consider it your new morning "Wake-Up Call," to reprogram your mind.

1. What thoughts usually come to your mind immediately upon waking up from sleep? Are

they positive and in support of you, your life, and your dreams and goals? Or are they filled with worry or stress about the day ahead?

2. How aware are you of the sensation when your feet first touch the floor as you arise out of bed? Consider injecting an affirming thought regarding your desired habit as you stand up to face the day.

3. What personal reminders and motivational messages can you set up for yourself throughout your day to reinforce your new habit? Be sure to keep these constant and refresh in your mind as you go about your day, as well as right before going to sleep at night.

Chapter 9

Optimism: The Biology of Hope

When we talk about faith and belief, we have to turn to the Scriptures, "Go your way; and as you have believed, so let it be done for you." That simple statement cuts both ways like a two-edged sword or a lock and key. *Belief is the key that can unlock the right door for everyone*—the means for getting rid of the lock that imprisons people, keeping them from ever knowing success. Belief is a power that everyone has but few consciously use. No individual possesses more of it than any other.

Therefore, the question isn't whether we have faith, it's whether we use it correctly. Belief, as a positive force, is the promise of realizing things hoped for and unseen. As a negative force, it is the premonition of our fear in an unseen darkness. Many people lead lives of quiet desperation having many days and nights spent in a state of anxiety.

There's no such thing as an absence of faith. It's always one kind or another. Optimism, or cynicism and despair. Much has been written for centuries about the *self-fulfilling prophecy.* A self-fulfilling prophecy is a statement that is neither true nor false, but that may become true if believed.

Your Pharmacy Within

We have lectured and written about the fact that the mind can't distinguish between things real and things vividly imagined, which is why faith and belief are so important. For example, when our fears and worries turn into anxiety, we suffer distress. Distress activates our endocrine system, changing the production of hormones and antibodies. Our immune system becomes less active, our resistance levels are lowered. We become more vulnerable to bacteria, viruses, and other ever-present hazards. There is evidence that some forms of asthma are psychosomatic, more related to a smothering relationship with a doting parent called "smother love" than to outside allergens.

In some cases, pictures of goldenrod were enough to bring on attacks of hay fever. In many cases, what we expect to happen, what we believe will happen, makes it happen. The powerful loneliness and hurt associated with what we call a broken heart can indeed lead to heart problems. There is also an apparent link between bottled up emotions and the growth of some cancerous tumors. Some splitting headaches might be precipitated by being pulled in opposite directions. A rigid personality and suppressed rage have been identified as factors in some cases of arthritis.

No doubt you're familiar with the placebo effect. *Placebo* literally means, "I shall please." Placebos are inert substances given to some volunteers in a given study, while other volunteers are treated with experimental drugs, and the effect is tested by measuring the difference in response to the powerless placebo versus the drug.

For example, some of a group of volunteers who had just had their wisdom teeth extracted were given morphine to alleviate their pain. The others swallowed a placebo that they believed to be morphine. Many of the placebo recipients said they experienced dramatic relief from their pain. However, when a drug that blocks the effect of the endorphin that was given them, the pain returned almost immediately. The test confirms something very important. When a patient *believes* that he or she has been given a pain reliever, the brain releases chemicals to substantiate that belief, and in some cases, the brain produces chemicals previously inhibited or impaired in individuals with certain diseases.

Parkinson's disease patients were given a placebo that they were told was an anti-Parkinson's drug. As a result, their ability to move increased. Brain scans revealed that

The Neuro-Psychology of Winning

their brains became activated in the areas that control movement and that dopamine was being produced naturally by the brain's own pharmacy.

We share with many audiences a true story about a man named Nick. Nick, a strong healthy railroad yardman got along well with his fellow workers and was consistently reliable on the job. However, he was a deep pessimist who invariably feared the worst and one summer day, the train crews were told that they could quit their job an hour early in honor of the foreman's birthday.

When the other workmen left the site, Nick, the notorious worrier, was accidentally locked in an isolated refrigerated boxcar that was in the yard for repairs. He panicked. He shouted and banged until his voice went hoarse and his fists were bloody. The noises, if anyone heard them, were assumed to be coming from a nearby playground or from other trains backing in and out of the yard. Nick reckoned the temperature in the car was zero degrees. *If I can't get out,* he thought, *I'll freeze to death.*

He found a cardboard box shivering uncontrollably. He scrawled a message to his wife and family: "So cold, body getting numb. If I could just go to sleep, these may be my last words." The next morning the crew slid open the boxcar's heavy doors and found Nick's body. An autopsy revealed that every physical sign indicated that he had frozen to death, but the car's refrigeration unit was inoperative. The temperature inside was about 61 degrees and there was plenty of fresh air. Nick's fear had become a self-fulfilling prophecy. So *be careful what you believe and pretend—it may come to pass.*

Your Amazing Brain

Our brains are so amazing that they can be trained to create the opposite effect of the negative voodoo-like true story of Nick. It was a Saturday in November and Arnold Lemerand was taking a stroll. He heard some children screaming and hurried over to where they had been playing near a construction site. A massive cast-iron pipe had become dislodged and had rolled down on top of the children, pinning 5-year-old Philip Toth against the earth. The boy's head was being forced into the dirt directly under the huge pipe and certain suffocation appeared to be imminent.

Arnold Lemerand looked around, but there was no one to help him in the attempted rescue. He did the only thing he could. He reached down and lifted the 1,800-pound cast-iron pipe off Philip's head. After the incident, he tried again to lift the pipe and couldn't even budge it. His grown sons tried to move it, but they failed as well. In an interview later with the Associated Press, Lemerand, who was 56 at the time, said that he had suffered a major heart attack six years before. "I tried to avoid heavy lifting," he smiled, with a young boy's arms around his neck. I called him to verify the story and it was true.

We read about such miraculous power surges every so often, don't we? We hear of grandmothers lifting cars and firemen making impossible rescues in burning buildings, exhibiting superhuman strength. Those kinds of stories used to sound rather tall to me, since I've always been a man to check the source and document the advice that people give me as to its validity.

I began to learn about how the mind can affect the body and how our thoughts can give us a natural high or make us ill. I was in Sarasota, Florida, serving as president of the International Society for Advanced Education, a non-profit foundation formed by Dr. Jonas Salk and other leading health scientists, to study preventive medicine and a holistic approach to wellness. The society was sponsoring continuing medical education seminars in cooperation with the University of Pittsburgh, the University of Nebraska, Johns Hopkins University, Harvard University, and other medical schools.

Proven Natural

At some of the seminars many years ago, presenters described research documenting the existence of substances in our brains similar to morphine and heroin. More than 30 years ago, they located receptor areas in the brain that act as locks that only these unknown substances

Optimism: The Biology of Hope

would fit, like keys. It was discovered that our brains contained these keys in the form of natural hormones.

Several have been identified including encephalon, endorphin, beta endorphin, and dynorphin. All of these hormones serve as natural pain relievers, many times more powerful than morphine. Beta endorphin is 190 times more potent than morphine. Scientists already knew that hormones play an important role in regulating certain of our biological processes. Adrenaline is the hormone that enables us to fight or flee in the face of danger or in response to a call for peak physical performance. Insulin regulates the sugar levels in our blood. Later discoveries have proven that morphine-like hormones are being manufactured in our own bodies to block pain and give us a natural high.

In one test, using endorphins supplied by the Salk Institute, Japanese researchers injected minute amounts of the hormone into 14 men and women suffering intense pain from cancer. From a single injection, they all felt relief from their pain for one to three days. In another experiment, 14 expectant mothers were given endorphin during labor and all reported immediate and lasting pain relief and delivered normal babies.

You've no doubt heard of the vicious cycle in which one problem gives way to another problem, leading back to the first problem. *Negative thinking deprives the body of endorphins leading to depression, leading back to more negative thinking.* Now, let's reverse the process.

There is growing scientific evidence that positive mental attitudes and beliefs actually create a natural high to help the individuals withstand pain, overcome depression, turn stress into energy, and gather strength to persevere. Physical exercise also aids in this process.

Positive Mental Attitudes

In one related study, actors were wired to electrodes and connected to blood catheters. They were then asked to perform various scenes. When they portrayed characters who were angry or depressed or without hope, endorphin levels dropped, but when the scene called for emoting joy, confidence and love, endorphins increased dramatically. If our thoughts can cause the brain to release adrenaline from the adrenal glands to help a 56-year-old heart patient lift an 1,800 pound pipe off a boy's head, and if our thoughts can produce natural endorphins, even when we're acting out roles that are 50 to 190 times as powerful as morphine, isn't it possible for us to use the power of optimism in our everyday lives with the only side effect being happiness?

When people ask me why I'm so optimistic and high on life, I tell them, "I'm on endorphins," and they say, "It figures, we knew you were on something." Visualization can be used to improve health and well-being.

Dr. Gerald G. Jampolsky, a well-known psychiatrist from California, has had a great deal of success using healing

Optimism: The Biology of Hope

visualization with both children and adults.[2] He also used visualization to help students with learning disabilities. In a typical group session, Dr. Jampolsky told his young patients to put away their thinking minds and put on their seeing minds. He then instructed them to create a mental blackboard, complete with chalk and eraser. Anytime a child saw words or phrases such as "can't, impossible, ought to, should," and "if only" on the blackboard, he or she was instructed to mentally erase those words or phrases.

> ## Happiness is the only side effect of the power of optimism in our everyday lives.

Dr. Jampolsky then had the children think about their disease and try to imagine what it looks like. He helped them understand what it actually looks like in their bodies. He then helped the children form positive mental pictures

---

2. Gerald G. Jampolsky, MD (1925-2020) wrote several books including *Love Is Letting Go of Fear; Teach Only Love: The Twelve Principles of Attitudinal Healing; and Good Bye to Guilt: Releasing Fear Through Forgiveness.*

of their disease receding, and of themselves recovering. Obviously, this technique is a supplement, not a replacement for traditional medical treatment.

Some of the most dramatic work in visualization techniques to improve health that we have researched has been the work by O. Carl Simonton, MD. The Simontons Center was the first cancer center to acknowledge the importance of family and personal support and to include them in the treatment plan. The Simontons have been using visualization along with traditional medical therapy to treat seriously ill cancer patients. Their approach is to get the patient to accept the responsibility for his or her illness and the cure, and then teach the patient to utilize deep relaxation and visualization exercises.[3]

One basic technique is to see the cancer and then imagine an army of healthy white blood cells attacking it and carrying off the diseased cells. The patient sees him or herself becoming totally healthy again. The Simontons have had an impressive number of case histories of people who have experienced complete remission from supposedly incurable cancer after using their visualization methods.

Since the pioneering work of the Simontons and others in the field, the use of *guided imagery* as a process to consciously direct the imagination in therapeutic settings is widespread. Its effectiveness has been documented as an effective intervention and adjunct therapy for patients

---

3.   www.simontoncenter.com; accessed March 1, 2025.

dealing with chronic pain, cancer, cardiac and stroke recovery, immune disorders, PTSD, anxiety and depression.

> **What you visualize and internalize, you must realize, can materialize.**

What you visualize and internalize, you must realize, can materialize. Research done by the Yale School of Public Health and the National Institute on Aging found that young people who had positive perceptions about aging were less likely to have a heart attack or stroke when they grew older.[4] And another study confirmed that middle-aged and elderly people lived an average of seven years longer if they had a positive perception of aging.[5] How

---

4. Becca Levy, PhD, "Young People's Views of Aging Can Predict Their Heart Problems in Old Age," *Yale School of Medicine,* February 22, 2009; https://medicine.yale.edu/news-article/young-peoples-views-of-aging-can-predict-their-heart-problems-in-old-age/; accessed January 26, 2025.

5. Becca R. Levy, et al., "Longevity increased by positive self-perceptions of aging," *NIH National Library of Medicine,* August 2002; https://pubmed.ncbi.nlm.nih.gov/12150226/; accessed January 26, 2025.

does your lifestyle, your expectations, and your forecasting affect your own health and well-being?

Optimism, an Incurable Condition

Optimism is an incurable condition in the person with faith. Optimists believe that most disease, distress, dysfunction, and disturbance can be remedied. Optimists also are prevention- and wellness-oriented. Their thoughts and actions are focused on solutions, health, and success. They concentrate on positive outcomes and rewards rather than the penalties of failure.

What the mind harbors, the body manifests, which is especially important when you're raising children or leading a team. Focus on the well family and dwell on good health as the usual environment around your house. We have seen more psychosomatic illnesses in homes where the parents dote on and smother their children with undue concerns for their health and safety than in any other type of household. We believe in safety precautions and sound medical practice. We also believe that your worst or your best concerns will likely come to pass.

Through many decades of dealing with Olympic athletes, professional sports, franchises and companies, the highest performers invariably, have had the most optimistic daily environments. You may not get what you want in life, but generally speaking, you are much more likely to get what you expect. Positive self-expectancy brings positive benefits into being. The advice to "Whistle while you work," therefore, is more than just fairy tale talk from a Disney character. It's very sound medical and psychological counsel.

> **Positive self-expectancy brings positive benefits into being.**

Well-Being Principles

The following are specific principles that you should put into practice every day. By diligently acting on these principles, you can do more for your physical well-being than any number of pills from a bottle and at a much lower expense:

1. Learn to listen to your body.

Learn to distinguish between genuine requirements and mere wants or cravings. If you're out walking on a hot day and your throat is parched, you really need a drink of water and you should have one. But if you just happen to be passing through the kitchen and you're immediately drawn to the cookie jar, that's something else again. The desire for food, exercise, sleep, or entertainment can all arise from authentic needs or just as substitute forms of gratification, so don't fool yourself. Eat when you're hungry. Drink when you're thirsty. Sleep when you're tired, and make those decisions yourself. *Don't let a television commercial or an advertisement in a magazine make the decision for you.*

2. Live in the present moment.

Seize the day. You may have heard athletic coaches say, "Play one game at a time." It may be a cliche, but it has a solid core of truth. Unless you choose to endow the past with importance, events from the past have no reality and neither do fears or premonitions of the future. Everywhere we look in nature, the trees, the flowers, and the animals are all sharply focused on being exactly what they are in the present moment. If we can just learn that lesson, if we can just *let go of regret and fear, we can take a huge step toward physical and emotional health.*

3. Resist the ever-present temptations of anger and vindictiveness.

Everyone has a million good reasons to be angry, but healthy and successful people find equally compelling reasons to be calm and happy. The physiological effects of anger on the heart, for example, have been well documented; but even if anger weren't dangerous, it's still simply unpleasant for everyone. No one has our respect more than a person who can cultivate personal happiness amid the twists and turns of life's journey. It's a far greater attribute than the ability to make money, shoot a basketball, or win an election. *Cultivate contentment and let go of anger and you'll live longer—and more importantly, you'll live well.*

4. Take off your judgment hat.

At some level, each of us feels we ought to rule the world. As kings and queens of creation, we would quickly straighten out everybody's mistakes and put things into good order. We all feel this way, but *the wisest and healthiest of us recognize those feelings as childish and superficial impulses.* We should also notice how these judgmental feelings increase in direct proportion to the dissatisfaction and frustrations that we experience in our own lives.

Positive Action Ideas

To add to those principles are some action ideas for more positive self-expectancy:

1. Optimism and realism go together.

Optimism and realism are the problem-solving twins. Pessimism and cynicism are the two worst companions. Your best friends should be individuals who are the "no problem, it's just a little temporary inconvenience" type. As you help other people in need on a daily basis, also develop an inner circle of close associations in which the mutual attraction is not sharing problems or needs. *The mutual attraction should be values and goals.* Resist the temptation to waste time reading or watching the sordid details of someone else's tragedies. Listen to inspirational music or instructional audios in your car. If possible, have breakfast and lunch with an optimist. Instead of sitting in front of the TV at night, spend time listening to and being involved with those you love.

2. Engage in positive recreation and education.

Select TV programs specializing in the wonders of nature, family health, and cultural enrichment. Select the movies and television you watch for their quality and story value rather than their commercial appeal. Change your vocabulary. Instead of saying, "I'm worn out," say, "I'm relaxed after an active day." Instead of, "Why don't they do something about it?" Make it, "I know what I'm going to do." Instead of group griping, try praising someone in the group. Instead of, "Why me, Lord?" Make it, "Try me, Lord." And instead of, "The world's a mess," say, "I'm getting my own house in order." *Get high on your expectations.* Instead of just wallowing away, have positive beliefs that will help you follow the way to the winner's circle. Remember, the people you associate, with the places you go, the things you listen to and watch, all are recorded in your thoughts.

3. Pass along your optimism.

Since the mind tells the body how to act, *think the highest and most uplifting thoughts that you can imagine.* Call, visit, text, email, or write to someone in need every day of your life. *Demonstrate your optimism by passing it on* to someone else and make your day of worship "good faith day." Get into the habit of attending your church, synagogue, mosque, or temple and do some honest listening and sharing. According to the most recent studies on drug abuse among teenagers and young adults, there are three cornerstones in the lives of those young individuals who do not use drugs of any kind—1) religious belief, 2) family and extended family relationships, and 3) healthy self-esteem.

As stressed throughout this book, you become what you think about most of the time. You become what you're most exposed—what you watch, what you hear, what you read, and your self-explanatory style have a profound influence on your outcomes in life. You are in control of the software program that runs your body and mind.

The future belongs to the optimist, to you.

Reflect and Connect

Consider the following statements to determine how optimism shows up in your life, and where you could make some positive changes. How strongly do you agree with each statement?

1. I compliment others often and express my appreciation for them.

2. Most of my comments to other people are positive.

3. I rarely criticize myself.

Optimism: The Biology of Hope

4. When I talk to myself, I use encouraging, helpful words.

5. Good things usually happen to me.

6. I always look for the good in people and situations.

7. I have a genuine interest in other people.

8. My friends are mostly positive thinkers.

Chapter 10

Resiliency: The Key to Success

Many years ago, there was a young musician who was slowly, but surely, going deaf. He realized that he would soon be unable to hear any music whatsoever—his own or anyone else's. He wrote in his will: "As the autumn leaves fall and wither; likewise, all my hopes have been destroyed. For Ludwig von Beethoven, at the age of 30, there seemed to be no reason to go on living.

If Beethoven's life had ended at that point, the cultural riches of the world would be greatly diminished and Beethoven, himself, would have forfeited the great triumphs that awaited him. But he, of course, did find the resiliency to go on living, and 23 years later his ninth symphony included lines from a poem titled, "Ode to Joy."

In all of Western classical music there is no composition that more emphatically celebrates love of life and deep affection for all of humanity. Somewhere between the despair of his early years and the great achievements of his maturity, Beethoven discovered emotional strength and physical endurance beyond anything he could have anticipated.

There's no doubt in my mind that you have the same inner strength, for every one of us has it. But if you're like most people there may be times when you've doubted this internal power; in fact, right now you may feel like there are situations in your life that are just as overwhelming. You may feel that your problems are even worse than Beethoven's and, anyway, he was an extraordinary person who had great talent to fall back on.

History provides us with many stories of gifted men and women who overcame difficulties, but it's not always easy to identify with such obviously unique individuals.

Well, let's look back at another example of personal resiliency on the part of a very different kind of person; but first let me explain where this example comes from.

Personal Resiliency

Probably the most valuable study ever done on personal resiliency was undertaken in the Hawaiian Islands on the Island of Kauai by two researchers named Emily Werner and Ruth Smith. This study—which followed more than 450 men from childhood through their adult lives—was an attempt to learn why some people are able to overcome

Resiliency: The Key to Success

severe disadvantages while others, from the same background, seem to have been overwhelmed by their problems.

In his book on *Ego Psychology,* Professor George Valiant, of the Harvard Medical School, refers to one of the subjects of this long-term study: a man Professor Valiant calls "Ken." Ken faced more disadvantages than almost all of the other 450 research subjects. He was by no means gifted in any conventional sense, with no particular talent or ability, and his IQ was well below the average.

Ken was born at the beginning of the great depression of the 1930s. His parents were divorced while he was still a baby and Ken was to be raised by his mother; but she died of alcoholism when he was four years old. He was then sent to an orphanage, where he remained until he was 12.

At that point he was taken to live with his paternal grandparents, but his grandmother suffered from severe mental illness and was frequently in the hospital. Ken's sister also had serious psychological problems and was hospitalized for 10 years. But things did improve somewhat for Ken when he was 13 and he went to live with his father.

At that point, Ken was interviewed by a social worker in connection with the research study that had been following the events of his life since his birth. Ken's answers to the interviewer's questions were really quite remarkable. Although he was well aware of the tragic things that had already befallen him, Ken found very positive things to say about his life.

In particular, he focused not on the early years but on the fact that he was now living in a household that was loving and secure. In describing Ken, at the age of 13, the researcher noted his ability to see both sides of situations and sway positive elements against negative ones. This, in fact, is an extremely important characteristic of resilient people and one that I strongly urge you to develop in yourself.

People who don't achieve the success that they had hoped for tend to see the world strictly in either-or terms; something is either all good or all bad, and most of the time such people see a lot more negative than positive aspects of the world.

The resilient person doesn't see life through rose-colored glasses; but resilient people do have the capacity to recognize life's complexities. The highly resilient Ken had developed this ability at the young age of 13.

Unfortunately, the difficulties in Ken's life didn't end with his childhood. However, he married and started a family; but his children died of a congenital blood disorder. Ken's marriage remained strong, though, and although he didn't achieve great financial success, he had a solid career in sales and marketing.

"Almost Miraculous"

When he was again interviewed for the study, in late middle age, the social worker who spoke with Ken described

Resiliency: The Key to Success

him as warm, generous, and completely without bitterness despite the numerous problems that he'd been called upon to overcome.

The interviewer wrote: "It's almost miraculous to see a man with many deprivations, almost from the beginning of his life, who has nevertheless emerged as such a picture of emotional and physical health."

Again, Ken was not a genius or especially gifted in any particular area, but he did have a sense of self-sufficiency and survivorship that seemed to have become quite rare in our own time. Ken resisted the tempting role of tragic victim, although for many years Nature seemed determined to cast him in that identity. Ken's resilience, his basic sense of self-esteem, and his ability to see good in others was described by the psychologist as a kind of invincibility.

As a child, his life seemed to be hopelessly broken and his future could have been described in almost dire terms—but he was the person who had the ability to put himself back together again. This is the kind of resiliency that psychologists have referred to as the "self-righting power of the human organism."

How Would You Answer
the "Big" Questions

Suppose you were asked to take someone on a mental journey through the events of your past. In what kind of light would you cast your life?

- Do you tend to view events in strictly positive or negative categories?

- Do you believe that people who disagree with your beliefs don't know the "truth"?

- How quickly do you bounce back from setbacks in your life?

- How do you approach obstacles that stand in the way of your goals?

- How have you successfully overcome them in the past?

- What personal traits or characteristics do you possess that make you more resilient?

- What traits or characteristics could you develop to enhance your resiliency?

The interpretation that you give to events is really more important than the events themselves. It's true: a lot of bad things may happen to good people, but there's a great deal of evidence that your ability to find the positive needle in the negative haystack is the most important key to success.

> # Your ability to find the positive needle in the negative haystack is the most important key to success.

As novelist William Faulkner once wrote: "The past certainly isn't over; in fact, it isn't even really past." What he meant, I think, is that the past never really ages. It's with us every second of every day. In fact, as we get older, it sometimes seems as if something you did years ago is more real than what you did yesterday.

The great philosopher and mathematician Alfred North Whitehead once made a fascinating observation. Whitehead wrote that "from a purely logical point of view, nothing is farther in the past than anything else; although our perception of time is like a road that we travel along. It's really more like a wall directly behind us. Once something goes behind the wall, it doesn't recede any farther. It's all in your mind and it can be reinterpreted and re-evaluated just like any other thought or feeling."

Your willingness to look at the events from your past in new ways is absolutely essential to developing a resilient character. Everyone has or will face adversity, challenges, or obstacles. The determining factor for your success in the coming years will be what will you do when the adversity comes? Will you persist, or panic? Will you murmur, or ponder? Will you look for reasons to push forward, or will you find excuses to quit and give up? Will you join the group griping and throwing themselves pity parties, or will you explore the opportunity that lies within the problem?

I've devoted much of my adult career studying the resilience of our returning prisoners of war (POWs) from World War II, the Korean War, and the Vietnam War. My years as a naval aviator led to lessons learned from survivors of the Holocaust, and then my work with astronauts.

More recently, as Chairman of Psychology, on the US Olympic Committee's Sports Medicine Council, I had the unique opportunity to see the thrill of victory and the agony of defeat up front, close, and personal. All of this, combined with my work with Superbowl and other professional sports teams were valuable in my understanding of what it takes to overcome any obstacle to survive and thrive.

When I encountered the Hawaiian study about resilience among ordinary individuals, like Ken, mentioned earlier in this book, I felt a special kinship to him. We both were born shortly after the Great Depression, from lower class families and broken homes. Our early lives were a series of roller coaster events, many of which were negative.

Authentic Resiliency

I've revealed publicly that my most profitable and noteworthy work, *The Psychology of Winning,* was written during one of the lowest points in my life, while I was losing in nearly every aspect of my life. However, it wasn't until several years ago that the demand for authentic resiliency paid me a sudden, unforeseen visit.

I had just returned from a month-long speaking tour throughout Asia, Europe, and the Middle East. A health checkup revealed that I had inherited a thickened heart valve condition from my mother. In my 80s, feeling good, I opted for a new heart valve so I could happily reach my goal of 100 golden years. Unfortunately, a surgical error severed my femoral artery and I nearly died on the operating table.

During recovery, I contracted a life-threatening infection in my new heart valve and spent three suspenseful months in isolated skilled nursing care. Just when I felt I had won this battle, I noticed a chronic sore throat, which was diagnosed as an acid reflux issue.

Nearly a year later, a biopsy revealed I had been misdiagnosed and actually was facing advanced-stage throat cancer requiring immediate, massive radiation and chemotherapy to save my life.

I rarely speak about my own pain and suffering, preferring to dwell on desired outcomes. Suffice to say that it has been the most brutal, indescribable experience imaginable:

- Internal and external radiation burns

- Cognitive challenges from chemotherapy

- Covid lockdowns in skilled nursing facilities

- Confined to a 9 by 12 room, with no visitors for months

- Too painful to swallow

- Then, unable to swallow

- Liquid diet only by feeding tube

- Taste buds destroyed

- Salivary glands inoperative

- Sleep deprivation

- Weight loss and muscle atrophy

And then, the moment of truth.

"Dig deeply into your resilience reservoir, Denis, and take charge. This is no drill. It's reality. Remember, this is a cake walk compared to what the POWs and wounded service men and women had endured."

Deborah~

And true to his words repeated in many books and countless lectures throughout his 50-plus years' career, I witnessed my dad not just "walking the talk," but *living* it, as he faced challenge after challenge of possible mortality with a resilience I have never known.

I remember seeing the van being loaded up with all his belongings to take him to a 6-month-long stay at a skilled nursing facility, to undergo intensive chemotherapy and radiation treatments, with no guarantee he'd make it through. I was overcome with tears of deep sadness and fear as I watched him preparing for his next big challenge, wondering if this might be the last time he'd be home.

But when the van finally disappeared beyond our driveway, I noticed my tears were becoming filled with some laughter—even joy, as I recalled his determined mindset, self-talk, dialogues with family, and instructions to the nursing facility staff:

"I will need a small desk in my room for my computer and laptop, and could you make sure I have wi-fi set up."

"No need for any hospital gowns, I will be bringing my own clothes and will be dressing myself."

"Please tell the housekeeping staff they do not need to make my bed. I get up at 5:30 every morning and do that myself.

"No need for a TV, I'll just need a little area for my weights, stretch bands and exercycle."

"No time for complaining, I need to start training."

"No time for stewing, I need to start doing."

And so his intentions became a reality. During that period, he finished writing *The New Psychology of Winning,* and nearly completed a draft for a second book, *The Psychology of Loving.* With speech therapy, he got his voice back. With swallow therapy, he learned how to swallow again. With physical therapy, he learned how to walk, without a walker. Even the doctors had been unsure of his capacity to survive this period.

Months later when he finally walked into their office, the first thing said to him was, "Hello Denis, I'm surprised to see you!"

Was this a miracle? Not really. Just someone being resilient when the chips are down.

BOUNCE BACK ABILITY

Our ability to bounce back after stressful events or challenging situations, while maintaining emotional equilibrium is the highly valued quality of resiliency. Individuals who possess self-resiliency effectively "ride out the storms" and learn from the challenges that life presents. They even seek out new experiences that provide them the opportunity to adapt to change in healthy ways, enhancing their well-being.

Did you know that the brain is actually the primary organ of resiliency? It regulates our biological feedback systems that respond or adapt to stress! We can adopt certain coping strategies that will promote resiliency including optimism, flexible thinking, and positive problem-solving, as we have discussed in previous chapters. Like the growth mindset, the resilient mindset, and additional skills we can develop will help us deal more productively to life's challenges.

As was mentioned earlier in this chapter, we each carry this same inner strength. You could say we are already "wired" for potential resiliency. Whenever or however challenging situations come our way, it is within our own choice and control, as to how we respond. Each time we meet an obstacle in our life, we have an opportunity to access and activate latent pathways of resiliency, until they become habits... the way we live our lives.

In my own life, at the age of 12, I was fortunate to learn about resiliency through misfortune when my family lost our home in a fire. In just a matter of minutes, we watched in horror as the security of the life we had known—all our possessions, belongings, necessities, and comforts—all gone. What had begun as sparks from a portable heater were now 70-foot-high flames, that by the time four fire engines arrived, had reduced our home to rubble.

The "blessings"—my mom, brothers, sister, and I, along with our dog, cats, hamsters, guinea pigs, parakeets, and turtles all made it out alive, and unscathed. My dad returned home from a tennis match in time to meet the fire trucks, news crew, and neighbors who had gathered in our cul-de-sac to witness the spectacle.

When asked the emotional question, "What on earth are you going to do now?" my dad simply answered, "We need to find a place to sleep tonight." And from that moment, I experienced sheer resiliency in action. The "goals" began to take shape and materialize—one day, one step at a time. Temporary places to stay, clothes, food, and transportation, and then a bank loan. Weeks after the fire, we were still digging through the charred rubble, in a futile search of my mother's wedding ring and any semblance of precious mementos or photographs.

We did gather pieces of melted furniture and remnants of fabric, which we made into a beautiful collage, that was later displayed in our town's contemporary art museum. We made the best of a devastating situation, and our family grew closer because of it. One year later, after an architect friend offered his services at a reduced fee to help design and rebuild a home for us, my parents threw a "House-Cooling" party to celebrate in gratitude for all those who saw us through our challenge.

It wasn't just a new home that had been built, it was also our resiliency. Just as our brains, after debilitating injuries and disease, can regenerate new cells and neuropathways within our bodies, and just as nature, herself, continually regenerates life through endless seasons and cycles, storms and devastations across our planet, we too, can do the same in our lives.

Reflect and Connect

Think back to a very challenging situation or experience you have encountered in your life—one that really tested your inner strength and resolve. Ask yourself the following questions:

1. What personal traits or characteristics helped me get through this tough time?

2. What specific self-talk and motivational messaging do I recall telling myself to help me push through or bounce back from adversity?

3. What did I learn from this experience that I could pass on as a gift to someone else going through a similar challenge?

Chapter 11

Empowerment and Relationships

W*inners empower others* *and build trust-ing relationships.* Winners project their best selves every day in the way they look, walk, talk, listen, and react. Winners specialize in truly effective communications. They take 100 percent of the responsibility not only for sending information or telling, but also for receiving information and listening for the real meaning from every person they contact.

Winners are aware that first impressions are powerful and that interpersonal relationships can be won or lost in about the first four minutes of conversation. Winners say, "I'll make them glad they talked with me." And to a winner you'll say, "I like me best when I'm with you." Nothing marks a winner so clearly as a relaxed smile and a warm face that volunteers his or her own name while extending a hand to yours, looking directly in your eyes and showing

187

interest in you by asking questions about your life that are important to you.

> # Winners value others.

Winners know that paying value to others is the greatest communication skill of all. A good way to think of leadership is the process of freeing your team members to do the best work they possibly can. More than anything else, today's business team members say they want the autonomy to do their jobs without the boss's interference.

Empowerment

In this fast-forward world, it's already clear that the best-run companies believe that the more power leaders have, the less they should use. *The key to authentic leadership is to listen to your followers and then open the door for them to lead themselves.* The secret is empowerment. The main incentive is genuine caring and recognition. The five most important words a leader can speak are, *"I am proud of you."* The four most important are, *"What is your opinion?"*

The three most important are, *"If you please."* The two most important are, *"Thank you."* And the most important single word of all is, *"You."*

In any of our relationships as leaders, managers, peers, colleagues, friends, parents, and significant others, positive messaging facilitates greater emotional buy-in. When we give others negative feedback in a non-positive manner, either verbally or non-verbally, we're actually reinforcing the negative pathways in their brains that cause negative behaviors in the first place.

When people are empowered to solve their own problems, their brains release a rush of neurotransmitters such as adrenaline. So a leader who *asks* rather than tells and who *guides and supports* rather than scolds and corrects, will be more effective. People learn best when they can go through a process of making their own connections and gaining their own insights. They will be more open to change and will welcome it if it is incremental and inter-active over time. And this is why studies show that while training programs alone may increase productivity by 28 percent, adding follow-up coaching can increase produc-tivity by up to 88 percent.

Motivation

To motivate individuals over an extended period of time, it's important to understand the psychology of human motivation. Basically, motivation can be external or internal. *External* motivation pulls you forward by some reward that you will attain by taking action. *Internal* motivation means doing something because it inspires your own sense of inner self-worth and contribution to society.

While both are important to achievement, intrinsic or internal motivation creates long-term commitment and loyalty more than simply the promise of external rewards. There are of course many successful entrepreneurs who are more money-motivated than in changing the world. There are equally as many successful entrepreneurs who are predominantly interested in improving the quality of life for others and who reap great financial rewards as a by-product of this vision of service.

We all want financial security. We all want to determine our own destinies. Most of us are motivated by material or external accomplishments to measure our success. However, money alone generally will not sustain loyalty or motivation.

There is a certain plateau or burnout point when money no longer motivates because a certain comfort level has been reached. Loyalty requires an inner force that compels commitment after standard of living needs have been met. Far too many people have disconnected their personal mission in life from their business or profession. The primary step in promoting loyalty is helping others define and pursue their own "magnificent obsessions."

A magnificent obsession is the way you want to live, not just the things you want to own. It is the person you want to be, not just the title you want after your name on your business card. A magnificent obsession is your mindset, not the degrees you earn. It is the worldview that you claim as your own, not the collection of stamps in your passport or photos in an album. Your magnificent obsession covers all areas of your life, including how you want to live, think, work, play, grow, create, worship, and to spend your precious hours, days, and years on this earth.

> # A magnificent obsession is your mindset, worldview— your overall lifestyle.

If it weren't for money, time, and personal responsibilities, what would you really love to do with your life? What do you really get excited about? Five years from now, what will your days be like? What will you be doing? Where will your focus be professionally? How will you be spending your time? With whom will you be spending your time?

Great leaders create loyalty by aligning their own visions for the future with the specific life goals of their followers. And this doesn't mean convincing others to follow the leader's vision. It does mean helping others define and reach their own individual magnificent obsessions via the same vehicle or business plan. Show a genuine interest in your team members' personal goals and interests, as well as their professional performance evaluations. Convince them by your actions that you have their interest and their successes in mind, not your own selfish motives that you are accomplishing through them.

Relationships

Especially when it comes to relationships, *keep your promises.* All true loyalties and long-term relationships are based on mutual trust. Break the trust and you break the relationship. Integrity is the cement that solidifies loyalty no matter what obstacles occur along the way. Empowered teams require a new communication style. In the old traditional work group, leaders wanted compliance. In an empowered team, leaders want initiative and innovation.

Directional communication such as announcing decisions, issuing orders, inhibits team input. If the team leader or supervisor is still using "boss language," the team gets the message that they're being told what to do. Managers of empowered teams need to learn to ask open-ended questions and develop the skill of truly listening to the answers.

Listening is a lost art, which must be rediscovered. Few people really listen to others usually because they're too busy thinking about what they want to say next. In business transactions especially, clear communication is often colored by power plays, one-upmanship, and attempts to press rather than to express in our work. This goes for our personal lives as well.

Listening

How we listen is at least as important as how we talk. Genuine listening to what others want allows more sales to be made, more deals to be closed, and greater productivity to be gained. Although it's not always necessary or possible to satisfy those wants, understanding them is the glue of a relationship. Not paying value by listening is a way of saying, "You are not important to me." The results are reduced productivity. Employees think, *I don't count here, so why should I even try?* Employee turnover results. *Who wants to work in a place where I don't feel valued?* Absenteeism. *I'm just a cog in the wheel only noticed when I make a mistake.* Retaliation. *They only listen when the griping gets loud enough.* Lost sales. *They don't seem to understand what I need.* And dangling deals. *I can't get through to them. It's like talking to a brick wall.*

The skill of listening, particularly *active* listening, is considered to be a critical leadership competency, yet not prioritized as much as it should be in corporate training programs. Research statistics prove that developing greater listening skills within the workforce have a profound impact on the bottom line:

- 80% of all workplace complaints and conflicts largely stem from poor communication, of which listening is a key component.

- Managers who received training in active listening have reported a 30% improvement in employee satisfaction.

- Active listening can increase collaboration and productivity by up to 25%.

- Individuals who are considered proficient listeners can achieve sales up to 42% higher than those who don't demonstrate good listening skills.

- Employees who feel heard are 4.6 times more likely to be empowered to excel.

Genuine listening can cure a remarkable range of supposedly intractable problems. If you have excellent presentation skills and have an authoritative and persuasive ability to speak to those you lead, make a conscious effort to convert your team meetings into creative dialogue where you ask open-ended questions and solicit feedback and input from all those present. Everyone can be a source of useful ideas. The people closest to the problem usually have the best ideas.

Learning flows up as well as down in the organization. Nothing is sacred except the governing vision and values. *The process of open dialogue improves performance.* The more information people can access, the better. Most importantly, don't view any suggestion or comment from the group as inane, silly, or irrelevant. Appearing foolish in front of one's peers is a major embarrassment and stifles any future desires to offer ideas that might be considered off the wall.

The most common mistake in communicating is saying what you want to say rather than what they need to hear, and then listening to what they have to offer. It's rightly been said that, "You can get more people to vote for you in 20 minutes by *showing interest in them,* than you can in 20 weeks by showing them how interesting *you* are."

No Matter What

When you think back in your life to the people you love and respect most, they have been the ones who have been there for you in person day in and day out no matter what. By actually considering your team as your own performance review scorekeepers, you'll spend the time and effort required to earn *their* respect by respecting *them* and keeping them informed of both the good and bad news ahead for the organization. Often those lowest on the pay or hierarchy scale are closest to the customer and therefore most aware of problems in delivering quality goods and services as advertised.

Having an active suggestion system in place that pays attention to and rewards innovation and making the organization more effective and efficient is crucial to success in a volatile competitive economy. David Ogilvy, founder of the giant advertising agency, Ogilvy and Mather, used to give each new manager a Russian doll, which contained five progressively smaller dolls inside. A message inside the smallest one read, "If each of us hires people we consider smaller than ourselves, we shall become a company of dwarves. But if each of us hires people who are bigger than we are, we will become a company of giants."

Instead of a numbers game, business today is truly a motivate-the-team game. In a global marketplace where the playing field is anything but level and where there is no job security because of slimmer profit margins due to outsourcing of manufacturing and service functions, it's imperative to *maximize the return on investment in the human capital already on your payroll.*

The following are nine steps to empowering team members:

1. Document their accomplishments so they can't pretend they don't exist. Never allow

team members to lose sight of their accomplishments and therefore their potential for success.

2. Show them how to find opportunity in adversity. Every outcome, no matter how negative, presents options that were not previously available.

3. Assign them tasks that display their talents. By transferring important responsibility to team members, you demonstrate your confidence in them and give them the chance to succeed in increasingly challenging assignments.

4. Teach them how to get what they want from other people. Teach your people to be assertive rather than too aggressive or too passive.

5. Show them the awesome power of listening, an active strategy for achieving personal success. When your subordinates become better listeners and begin reaping the benefits, they'll feel better about themselves.

6. Tell them exactly what you expect of them and find out what they expect of you. The reason most subordinates and team members give for not satisfying their management is not knowing what management expects.

7. Critique performance, but not people. The spirit of criticism should be, "I don't like what you did in this case, but I do like you."

8. Praise not only them, but also their performance. You don't want merely to keep your people happy. You want them to know what they did right so they can repeat it.

9. Keep them in ongoing training and coaching programs. This gives them a vote of confidence, and carefully chosen training and coaching will further contribute to their effectiveness. As accomplishments mount, self-confidence and ability grow in other areas as well. The more we accomplish, the larger our view of our enormous capacity for creative growth.

It has been said that there are no business problems that aren't really people problems that impact business decisions and outcomes. Solicit feedback from the bottom up rather than make edicts and policies from the top down. To become a giant in the eyes of others and to succeed in the 21st century, *look up to those beneath you.*

Empowerment and Relationships

> # Total success is the continuing involvement in the pursuit of a worthy ideal.

Total success is the continuing involvement in the pursuit of a worthy ideal, which is being realized for the benefit of others rather than at their expense. And success is the process of learning and sharing and growing. Learn how others feel and consider where they're coming from before criticizing or passing judgment. Even if you can't emotionally feel for everyone you meet with sympathy, be certain that you understand how others feel with empathy. The best leaders and managers in the world look for value and pay value often to members of their team. Their motto: *If you win, I win too.*

Develop that caring touch. Reach out today and tonight and tomorrow and every day for the rest of your life and give someone the value of your attention. Remember, a touch is worth a thousand words or text messages. Text messages are the most impersonal forms of communication. They are the enemy of intimacy. Your personal physical presence, being there with your employees and being there with your loved ones.

The most important motivational message in the world is, "I'm here for you because I care for you. You're worth my full attention right now." Being in person to encourage and support others is the ultimate expression of empowerment and the key to enduring relationships.

Reflect and Connect

Consider your current relationships that are most meaningful to you, and the people whose lives you could positively impact. Then answer the following questions:

1. How much of an effort do you make to foster these relationships on a regular or periodic basis?

2. When you interact with these people in your life, how aware are you of what is important to them? What their perspective is, and/or where their thoughts and views are coming from?

3. How good of a listener are you? Or do you mostly listen with your own agenda in mind?

Chapter 12

A Glimpse Into the Future

O f all the wisdom we have gained throughout our lives, the knowledge that time and health are taken for granted until they are depleted has caused us to reorder our daily priorities. As with health, time is the raw material of life. We can bide our time, but we can't save it for another day. We can waste and kill time, but we are also mortally wounding our opportunities.

Time is the ultimate equal opportunity employer. Each human being has exactly 168 hours a week to spend. Think about it! Scientists can't invent more minutes. Super-rich people can't buy more hours.

We worry about things we want to do but can't, instead of doing the things we can do but don't. It is not the experience of today that causes us the greatest stress. It is the regret for something we did or didn't do yesterday, and the apprehension of what tomorrow may bring.

Early in this book we suggested that technology has enabled the bombardment of our senses 24/7 with what appear to be insurmountable problems faced by all living things on our planet. This daily diet of what's wrong in this tumultuous world creates an atmosphere of frustration, helplessness, and fear of the future.

In Chapter 1 we acknowledged that media purveyors are paid well to serve up what sells. They know that the need to be shocked or viscerally stimulated is greater than the need to be informed or inspired. This same psychology is what makes a crowd gather at a fight or an accident.

Fashion does not imitate real life. Life imitates fashion. The media shape our patterns of eating, sleeping, dressing, and recreation. They help form our values, morals, professional goals, social behavior, and perceptions of the real world. We learn by observation, imitation, and repetition. We seize upon role models, observe their actions, imitate, and then become what we see, hear, read, feel, and touch. No single realization is as important as this in understanding and dealing with your brain and mind.

Catastrophes dominate all forms of media through video streaming almost in real time. It is difficult to determine what are AI-generated stories, fake stories, or actual events. As a result, we are polarized politically, culturally, regionally, and globally.

Who do you trust today to give you the facts?

The Dawning of a New Era

In the time it takes you to read this current page, approximately ten new scientific papers are being published in professional journals around the world, announcing research that advances or contradicts previous information. It is nearly impossible to determine the speed in which tech companies or start-up teams around the globe are suggesting new breakthroughs in some life-enhancing innovation or technology. And the pace of accelerating knowledge is increasing exponentially.

The obsolescence of typewriters, fax machines, desktop computers, camera film, video and audio tapes, compact disks, and telephone landlines used to be gradual, over a several-year period. Today, we are offered advanced smart phones every year. Even our wristwatches, rings, and other wearable accessories have become our personal bio-computers.

> There are more changes in one of our days than in a decade of many of our grandparents' lives.

The fields of Artificial Intelligence (AI) and quantum computing have witnessed remarkable advancements that promise to revolutionize virtually every aspect of our daily lives, particularly healthcare. These technologies, when combined, have the potential to enhance efficiency, accelerate research, and ultimately lead to better health outcomes.

While we depend on our grandchildren to help us with simple tech glitches in the most basic searches and programming of our smartphones and smart TVs, they will soon face the changes every week, that my generation faced once a year at most. How marvelous it would be if I could live long enough to experience the dawning of this new era in human development. My grandmother lived through the discovery of electricity, the automobile, radio, air travel, television, computers, and the moon landing.

Quantum computing holds the promise of carrying out calculations that would take today's systems millions of years and could unlock discoveries in medicine, chemistry, and many other fields where nearly infinite seas of possible combinations of molecules confound today's computers. Quantum computing, which harnesses the principles of quantum mechanics, enables the processing of vast amounts of data at unprecedented speeds. Unlike classical computers that use bits as the smallest unit of data, quantum computers utilize "qubits," which can represent and process multiple states simultaneously.

A Glimpse Into the Future

This capability allows them to tackle complex problems that are currently not possible for today's systems. For instance, in drug discovery, quantum computing can simulate molecular interactions at a level of detail that was previously unachievable. This acceleration in the drug development process can significantly reduce the time it takes to bring new medications to market, ultimately saving lives.

Artificial Intelligence (AI) has made significant strides in analyzing healthcare data, predicting patient outcomes, and personalizing treatment plans. Machine learning algorithms can sift through vast datasets, identifying patterns and correlations that human analysts might overlook. For example, AI can analyze medical images with high accuracy, assisting radiologists in detecting diseases such as cancer at earlier stages. The integration of AI in diagnostics not only enhances the speed of detection but also improves the accuracy of diagnoses, leading to timely interventions and better patient prognosis.

The combination of quantum computing and AI can lead to breakthroughs in personalized medicine. Quantum algorithms can process genetic information and other health data to identify the most effective treatments tailored to individual patients. This level of personalization can optimize treatment efficacy while minimizing adverse effects, ultimately improving patient outcomes and saving time in trial-and-error approaches to medication.

AI-driven health monitoring systems, powered by quantum computing, can revolutionize preventive healthcare. Wearable devices that continuously monitor vital signs can analyze data in real-time, alerting patients and healthcare providers to potential health issues before they escalate. This proactive approach can significantly reduce hospital visits and improve overall health management.

Having endured more than seven years of trial and error diagnostics regarding my health and quality of life issues, I am enthusiastic about the speed of technological advances. By the time you read this book, many of these research efforts will have already been adopted as standard practices in many industrialized nations. The following are a few we found as particularly noteworthy:

Brain-Computer Interfaces (BCI)

This technology is experiencing rapid growth within the field of neuropsychology, with significant real-world applications. Recent breakthroughs are enabling direct communication between our human brain (our thoughts) and external devices (physical reality).

- Elon Musk's Neuralink, a tiny electrode brain implant, has achieved successful results in human clinical trials begun in 2024, by allowing individuals with severe motor impairments to control digital devices purely through their thoughts.

- Synchron has developed a precision brain implant, called a stentrode, which is inserted through the bloodstream, allowing paralyzed patients to regain control over computers, giving them more communication and independence.

- Researchers at Stanford University have developed an AI-assisted BCI that allowed patients with full-body paralysis to translate their thoughts to actual words being typed onto a computer screen.

- Applications for faster decision-making, enhancing focus, reaction time, and cognitive resilience, as well as faster language acquisition and stress resistance, are being funded by the US Defense Advanced Research Projects Agency (DARPA).

Brain-to-Brain Interfaces (BBI)

Recent academic and research developments toward the practical application of this field are showing promise:

- In February 2025, the National Science Foundation began funding a grant to Northern Illinois University's College of Engineering and Engineering Technology for the development of a two-way brain-to-brain interface that will facilitate direct communication between individuals without verbal or physical interaction. This technology will use advanced brain imaging, EEGs, and brain stimulation modalities.

Non-Invasive Brain Stimulation (NIBS)

The use of these techniques that influence brain activity through the use of electrical or magnetic fields, without the necessity of surgery, have far-reaching effects in neurological therapy, cognitive enhancement, and psychiatric treatment.

- An AI-driven Transcranial Magnetic Stimulation (TMS) therapy has been developed to significantly improve treatment-resistant depression in patients. This allows for a treatment based on customized stimulation patterns of a patient's brain activity.

- Transcranial Alternating Current Stimulation (tACS) has been successful in improving memory and cognitive function in older adults, with a 2024 study demonstrating that 10 minutes of treatment enhanced memory performance for up to 1 month.

Virtual Reality Therapy (VRT)

Significant advancements are being made in the application of VR therapy for psychological treatments. Best suited for use with professional mental health clinicians, positive results are being achieved in treating anxiety, depression, phobias, and post-traumatic stress disorders (PTSD). The use of Virtual Reality simulations for corporate coaching and development is gaining traction in the training of soft skills, technical skills, onboarding, and stress management.

VR provides realistic immersive environments and through simulation, creates engaging experiences to enhance learning. Overcoming the fear of public speaking, or a lack of confidence when presenting to, or interacting with, a group of people, is an area where VR training can glean immediate positive results in communication effectiveness.

Time Effectiveness and Efficiency

In addition to all of the breakthroughs in the health fields, Artificial intelligence (AI) is increasingly enhancing human cognitive capabilities, offering tools that augment memory, learning, and problem-solving skills. These advancements are reshaping how we interact with technology and how technology, in turn, supports our mental functions.

The Neuro-Psychology of Winning

- **Cognitive Offloading:** This is a term that will affect our everyday lives in amazing ways. AI systems, such as virtual assistants and chatbots, allow individuals to delegate routine cognitive tasks, thereby reducing mental load and freeing up cognitive resources for more complex activities. It will be like having our own "genie" at our command day and night.

- **Enhanced Learning and Memory:** AI-driven applications are being developed to improve working memory and task-switching abilities. For instance, training in real-time human-AI interaction has been shown to enhance cognitive functions in language professionals, suggesting potential benefits across various fields.

- **AI-Augmented Creativity:** AI tools are increasingly used to augment human creativity, assisting in generating new ideas and solutions across various domains. This collaboration between human intuition and AI's data processing capabilities leads to innovative outcomes.

- **Organoid Intelligence (OI):** Researchers are exploring the use of lab-grown brain organoids combined with AI to create biocomputing systems. This emerging field aims to develop computing platforms that mimic human brain functions, potentially leading to more efficient and powerful cognitive processing systems.

- ***AI-Driven Personalized Education:*** The integration of AI in educational settings is expected to revolutionize learning by providing personalized experiences tailored to individual cognitive styles and needs. AI can adapt educational content in real-time, optimizing learning efficiency and retention. In the United States, we spend more per pupil on education, yet find ourselves near the bottom in educational proficiency among all developed nations.

While these advancements hold significant promise, they also raise ethical considerations, particularly concerning cognitive offloading and the potential dependency on AI systems. Balancing AI assistance with the preservation of our own critical thinking and problem-solving skills is essential to ensure that AI serves as a tool for enhancement rather than a crutch leading to cognitive and creative atrophy. Emotional intelligence is the thread that is woven throughout the fabric of all synergistic human cultures. Without it, no society has ever survived its own, brief success.

The Evolution of our *Human* Consciousness

The evolution of human consciousness is moving toward deeper self-awareness, inner alignment, and a greater sense of interconnection. Grounded in advances in neuroscience, epigenetics, and energy medicine, practices like mindfulness, meditation, somatic therapies, and integrative psychotherapies are helping us map new inner terrains. Expanding consciousness is not just a mental shift—it's a holistic integration of heart, mind, body, and spirit that honors both personal transformation and collective flourishing.

A growing number of universities and research organizations are exploring and advancing our understanding of the nature, evolution, and potential future developments in human consciousness. The following are just a handful:

- *University of Arizona – Center for Consciousness Studies:* Interdisciplinary programs are offered in the scientific and philosophical perspectives of the nature of consciousness.

- *University of Wisconsin-Madison – Center for Healthy Minds:* Founded in collaboration with the Dalai Lama to research neuroplasticity, compassion, emotional resilience, and mindfulness training.

A Glimpse Into the Future

- ***Stanford University – Stanford Center for Compassion and Altruism Research (CCARE):*** Works with neuroscientists, psychologists, and spiritual teachers to explore how compassion can be trained through meditation and breathwork.

- ***University of Oxford – Oxford Centre for Neuroethics:*** Investigates consciousness, free will, and mind enhancement using neurophilosophy and brain-mapping technology.

- ***Harvard University – Program in Placebo Studies and Therapeutic Encounter:*** Studies how beliefs, imagination, and perception influence healing and reality through the placebo effect.

- ***HeartMath Institute – Heart-Brain Communication:*** Research emphasizes the importance of how the heart influences the brain, specifically in sending signals that impact perception, emotion, and cognitive function.

Artificial Intelligence can become a powerful ally in the evolution of our consciousness—not as a replacement for our Authentic Intelligence (the other AI), but as a mirror and amplifier of it. If used consciously and guided by human values, Artificial Intelligence has the potential to expand learning, spark creativity, reveal patterns, and foster collaboration.

But it is crucial that we use AI technology to support, not suppress, our full potential. If we outsource too much of our thinking, feeling, or creativity, we risk becoming disconnected from our inner wisdom. True progress comes when we combine our own imagination and inner knowing with technology to elevate human awareness, not diminish it—co-creating a future grounded in compassion, vision, and wholeness.

As psychology, neuroscience, biology, quantum physics, sociology, ecology, and spirituality increasingly come together, their integration is giving rise to powerful new paradigms. These emerging frameworks will not only challenge our current ways of thinking but also invite us to enhance our awareness and commit to a more elevated, interconnected way of living and being.

> **When one life changes course, the whole current of humanity begins to transform.**

A New Tipping Point

Turning points and tipping points create significant crossroads in our evolution. A turning point is often a moment of conscious decision—when we break a pattern, overcome an obstacle, choose a new direction, or rise to meet our potential. A tipping point, on the other hand, is the unseen threshold where enough small shifts accumulate—some conscious, some not—until a dramatic transformation takes place. While history often remembers the external tipping points, true evolution begins with the quiet revolution within individual lives.

This is where your true "winning" arises. We have two choices in our lives: curse the darkness or seek enlightenment. We can accept the external forces over which we have little or no control; or we can assume the responsibility for being a catalyst for positive change in our own daily actions. Every time you choose to turn toward courage, authenticity, or optimism, you contribute to the growing current of collective change. When many make that turn, the system itself begins to bend. But when we retreat in fear, give in to self-doubt, or abandon our own path, we don't just delay personal growth and achievement, we withhold a vital strand in the larger tapestry of human evolution. Personal turning points become global turning points when enough people live their truth consistently and visibly.

Lasting change doesn't cascade from the top down—it ripples from the inside out. And this is how humanity reaches a new tipping point; not through one great event, but through the steady turning of countless individuals committed to fulfilling their potential in service to something greater than themselves.

> # Could commitment be that turning point in your life when you seize the opportunity to alter your destiny?

This We Believe

Despite the stark realities that we have endured throughout human history and that continue to foster discouragement and doubt about lessons learned and mistakes repeated, there are reasons to be hopeful, even thrilled. The human spirit is alive and well. We have proven to be seekers as well as sufferers. We are adventurous, curious, courageous, and bold. While obstinate and stubborn to a fault, we revel in being change agents, rather than accept our status as change victims.

We question our purpose during our short lifespans. We question the size and origins of our universe and wonder what lies beyond our current theories and telescopes. We ponder about life on other planets and whether space travel is science fiction or fact, or if travel throughout inner space may be even more vast, exciting...or necessary. We are beginning to understand how little we know about the universe residing inside each of us, between our right and left ears, and somehow present within every cell of our body—that unique human brain gifted with an unlimited creative imagination, capable of turning dreams into reality.

Every marvelous, breathtaking invention and innovation created by humans since our beginning have resulted from unbreakable optimism and faith in our future. We must not forget—not for a single day, or even a single moment, that no matter what obstacles or challenges life throws our way, we are already programmed with the capacity to not just survive, but also thrive.

Live each day as if it were your last, not in the future, not in the past. You may not get what you want, but in the long run, you will get what you expect.

The winners in life think constantly in terms of *I can, I will, and I am.*

This we believe. Do you?

Reflect and Connect

Think back on key chapters or ideas that had the most impact on you. Capture your thoughts and reflections as soon as possible—perhaps write in a journal or record on your phone.

1. What is calling for your immediate attention?

2. Where do you feel the strongest desire to take action?

3. What is one thing you could start doing or thinking?

4. How ready and willing are you to begin?

There is no better time in your life, than NOW!

About the Authors

Denis Waitley & Deborah Waitley, PhD

Recognized as a pioneer in the personal development industry, Denis Waitley has painted word pictures of optimism, core values, motivation, and resiliency that have become indelible and legendary in their positive impact on society. His books, keynote lectures, audio and video programs, and seminars have impacted thousands of individuals and organizations globally, and have been translated into 14 languages. He has studied and counseled leaders in every field, including Apollo astronauts, heads of state, Fortune 500 top executives, Olympic gold medalists, and students of all ages and cultures.

Deborah Waitley, PhD, is a distinguished change agent specializing in leadership development and performance enhancement. With extensive experience working with Fortune 500 companies, multinational corporations, and small businesses worldwide, she is known for driving mindset innovation and applying cutting-edge neuroscience techniques to achieve organizational success and growth.

As president of her consulting firm, Waitley Global Enterprises, and The Waitley Institute (founded by her father, Denis Waitley), Deborah integrates her strong background in psychology to train, coach, and consult for optimum results in workforce motivation and synergistic team building. She holds certifications in biofeedback technology, emotional intelligence (EQ), and virtual reality therapy (VRT). She has created an online, self-directed coaching program "The NeuroPsychology of Winning," based on this book, as well as other programs designed to activate and realize your authentic intelligence and innate potential.

OTHER BOOKS IN
The Waitley Institute Collection

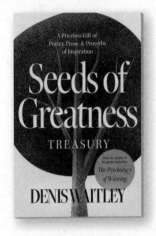

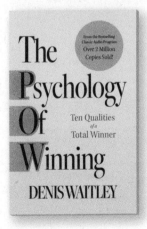

AVAILABLE WHEREVER BOOKS ARE SOLD

THANK YOU FOR READING THIS BOOK!

If you found any of the information helpful, please take a few minutes and leave a review on the bookselling platform of your choice.

BONUS GIFT!

Don't forget to sign up to try our newsletter and grab your free personal development ebook here:

soundwisdom.com/classics